MY JOURNEY TO FREEDOM AND FAITH

by Aina F. Torell

Endorsement

Knowing the autthor since 1971 as a personal friend of mine as well as a sister in Christ, I have learned to know Aina Torell as a devoted, spirit-filled, gifted Christ-like Christian. She has been used by God in a number of situations to administer the power of God to people in need, as well as practice an outstanding faith based on the Word of God. I definitely recommend this book to anyone, whether a believer or not. The reader will not want to stop reading until reaching the last page.

Owen Bergh

Acknowledgments

I would like to first thank my Heavenly Father for helping me to write my story. To Him belongs all honor and glory.

I also want to thank my husband who was led to write an article about A. A. Allen on our website many years ago, and a lady evangelist by the name of Jacqueline D. Jones responded with a nice letter to my husband. She was deeply touched by his writings about A.A. Allen and other things. To our amazement she also sent a copy of her recently published book by CSN Books along with their catalog.

I had a bad experience when I contacted a graphic art and publishing company, so I was praying that God would help me to find a good publisher. When I saw the catalog, I was very excited and after contacting them, I decided to send in my manuscript for review. I am happy to state that they decided to publish my book.

I also want to thank my sister's in the Lord, Carol West and Sharon McDaniel who expressed such joy over the manuscript. With great appreciation I thank my nephew's Charles and Joshua for their help. I also want to thank another sister in the Lord, Lynne Cardwell, for her support.

Table of Contents

Chapter One

My Childhood Years

I was doing my daily housework when the phone rang and the thought came to me, "Who needs help now?" Being a minister's wife had prepared me to expect the unexpected, so I asked God for wisdom as I answered the phone. To my surprise and joy it was Bridget, a young Christian lady who at an earlier time had visited our church service. Now she wanted to share something with me. She told me that she had written to Channel 19, a television station in Modesto, and had recommended that John and I be on their program. We finished our conversation and I thanked her and said, "May God's will be done."

When I began to seek God's leading in this matter, Jesus reminded me of the time when I accepted Him as my personal Savior and Lord. I got really excited when I thought about how Jesus could use my testimony for His glory on TV even though I had no television experience. The TV station sent us an application to fill out; we answered all the questions they asked of us, and gave them the information they needed. It wasn't long before we received an answer from them stating that they would like us to be on their program.

As I prepared myself to go on television, my thoughts went back to my childhood in a small town, called Vedum, in Sweden. Is this the little girl who had walked the streets of that town so many times, yet never for a minute thought that one day she would not only move to America, but also be on TV? This girl was now a woman who had given her life to the Lord. My husband and I were not only saved, but we had also been called into full time ministry.

God opened many doors for John and I to evangelize in many different countries, especially in Sweden. As my husband and I held evangelistic crusades, there were several interviews for various papers, both Christian and non-Christian. There were many big write-ups about us, and the meetings we were having. Many people had been saved, filled with the Holy Spirit, and healed in a mighty way by Jesus. Also miracles were taking place in a most unusual way. But to be on TV was completely new for me, and this was to be aired live.

I felt led to pray for both my husband and I as we took off for the trip to the TV station in Modesto. When we arrived we were met with a nice smile by the host for our program, Laurian Bettencourt, and I felt somewhat at ease.

As John and I walked toward the set, I felt my heart pounding very hard, but at the same time I felt the Holy Spirit guiding us as we told our personal testimonies. Immediately after the interview, the phones at the TV station started to ring and we were able to minister to those people who wanted to talk to us.

My Birth and Childhood

I was born in Vedum, a small town in the southwest area of Sweden. Judit Everet, the midwife, was God's choice to help my mother deliver a set of twin girls into this world. I don't think the midwife knew that our mother was going to have twins. My mother had a very rough time during the childbirth. First of all, I was much bigger than my twin, and I came out bottom first which caused my twin sister Daga to be squeezed inside the womb. The midwife was very concerned that my twin sister wouldn't make it, and did everything to save her life. She succeeded with the Lords help. Daga came out two hours later, but since she didn't have much oxygen In the womb, when she came out she was completely blue in her face. Another reason for her blue face was how long childbirth took for a set of twins. My twin sister was classified as a blue baby because of the circumstances even if she had no problem with her heart. After all the agony and pain, our mother was completely exhausted but happy that everything was over. She was a very kind mother, and she really proved to us how much she loved us through the years.

Talk about day and night! I had very blond hair and my twin had dark brown hair. We were not alike at all, but we looked like sisters. I was born at 2:00 a.m. weighing 7 lbs 8 oz. My twin sister decided to come into this world at 4:00 a.m. weighing 3 lbs 15.5 oz. They called her Daga, and they named me Aina. Outside it was 8 degrees Fahrenheit. This was cold! There were 8 inches of snow outside. Because Daga was a blue baby, the midwife was very concerned if she was going to make it, but she did! Many years later I found out from my mother that when Daga's life was in a very critical condition, I refused to eat very much. Before long she increased her weight, and later she became bigger then me.

As my twin sister and I grew up we were very close and had many happy times together as well as with our sister Vally, who was only one year older than us. My grandmother on my mother's side passed away before we were born. My mother was the only child. Grandfather died sometime later.

Our parents, Helge and Valborg Strom, had a farm, located in a little village called South Lundby, which was about 3.5 miles outside the town of Vedum.

Our childhood years were peaceful and carefree until I was one year and four months old and World War II broke out; I could sense my parents' sorrow, uncertainty and fear. Although Sweden was neutral, there was no guaranty that it would stay that way. Before long my dad was drafted into the army, after which we didn't see him very much.

I was the first one to walk, and the first one to try a bike ride. Vally had got a brand new children's bike, but she had such fear, so our dad had to help her and that took some time before she was able to ride a bike for herself. The first time I was biking, I took my mother's bike. I fell down and scraped my knees, but I got up again and was able to handle that big bike. Later on my twin sister and I got our own bikes, and Daga was able to learn how to handle her bike very well.

My father was in the army, and stationed in the northern part of Sweden. In the winter time there was lots of snow and it was very cold. He told us how at one time he had to take a frozen dead body on his truck for many miles. The body belonged to a German pilot who had crash landed on a frozen lake. After they got him up from the lake, my dad had to take the body during the night to its final destination. That was a very uncomfortable experience for him.

During the time that my dad was in the army, our mother had to take care of her three girls and also attend to the farm. She had some help from time to time, and sometimes she would have a baby-sitter for us, but not very often. While we were growing up we didn't have many toys, so we used our imagination. Sometimes we would play that we had a store. Our older sister Vally was the owner of the store, and my twin sister Daga and I were the customers. Since we used different kinds of herbs for various purposes, we often brought violets, and other flowers picked from the field, to our mother.

Dad Home on Short Leave

When my father was home on a short leave, my parents would sometimes turn the radio on. I can still remember the angry voice of Adolph Hitler booming out from the airwaves. I sensed a tremendous evil coming from that man. We were happy to have our dad home, but too soon he had to leave us again and we were heartbroken.

Life went on, and one day when I was a little girl I scared my mother half to death. I decided I was going to take a closer look at our neighbor's big bull. I climbed over the big fence, and went over and petted him. Mother somehow got me away from him, but needless to say I never saw the bull that close again. I didn't have any fear of animals at all. In fact, as I grew older I had a special touch and ability with animals that could only have come from God. I didn't know that God had given me a gift, even though I wasn't saved.

Our mother had a box that was filled with beautiful cards from America. She had received those from relatives that lived in different places in the United States, and she treasured them very much. Mother tried very hard to hide them high up in the attic, but since I loved to climb all over the place I always managed to take them down and we girls had a great time playing with them.

End of the War

The war was finally over in 1945, and our dad came home for good. We were all very happy about that. We loved Dad, but I noticed that he changed after he had come home from the army. We were about six to seven years old. He had become strict, and was very angry when he spanked us. That created in all of us fear and insecurity.

I remember one time we had gone over to the neighbors. They had a children's party, and our dad wanted us to come home at a certain time. In the beginning we checked the clock, but then we got so involved in playing that we forgot the time until one of us looked at the clock. We were horrified when we saw how late it was, and we ran home very fast. When we came home, our mother told us that Dad was very angry and we better hurry and go to bed, which we did. The room was upstairs. I have no recollection of what happened after this. Our mother told us before we went to bed that Dad had gone to the neighbors looking for us. We had taken a short cut home. I remember when we were very small he would take us up and give each one of us a hug and he looked very happy at those times. We were sad about what the war did to our dad. Later we found out that, in the army, he had been exposed to poisonous gas, which caused headaches.

One thing we girls did very early was to sing. Sometimes our parents would have people come to the farm to help them in their work, and they taught us many songs, most of them folk songs. Very often, Dad would play the organ and have us sing with him. Although we were not very old at the time, he seemed to enjoy it very much. Our mother played the organ also and sang, but not very often. When she did sing I always wanted to hear her sing *"When the Lord Creates a Flower."* She had a nice voice and played very beautifully, but her work at the farm and taking care of us took all her time, unfortunately.

I was about 6-7 years old when my mother decided to take me with her to a friend who was living in Vedum. We were still living in the small village called South Lundby at that time. It was day time, but it was also wintertime, and it was cold. We were dressed up in very warm clothing. My mother was taking her bike, and she put me on the back of the bike just behind her seat. After some time it began snowing and it was not easy for mother, but she had promised her friend to be there with her. We made the six kilometers safely to her place.

Her friend was happy to see us and there was plenty of food and cookies, which tasted better than ever. My mother and her friend had not seen each other for a long time so they were talking up a storm, and I was kind of bored. This lady's apartment was on the second floor so I decided to go down the stairways; I didn't realize by that time it had become much darker, I couldn't see very clearly. My feet slipped and I went rolling like a ball down the stairway. Needless to say, I made quite a noise when I finally landed on the first floor, and the neighbors downstairs came out looking very scared. My nose was bleeding tremendously and there was blood all over.

If I recall it correctly, my mother and her friend came down the stairways in a hurry, and they carried me back up to the apartment. After some time they were able to stop the bleeding. I was born with a perfect straight nose, but after that accident it became crooked. It was late and apparently they could not get hold of a doctor; at that time they most likely didn't have what they have today to fix my nose, so I just learned to live with it. I have proof to show how I used to look on a picture before the accident. Was I ever joyful to be back in our home again!

My School Years

When my twin and I were seven years old, it was time for us to begin school. Our parents wanted me to wait another year because I was so tiny, but I put up such a fuss about that they finally gave in. In the beginning, going to school was very hard for me because we had to ride on our bicycles about 7 miles every day. It tired me, but I made it. We found out some years later that I had anemia. The doctor gave me some good natural herbs and I did very well after that.

One day in school, when we had physical education and were playing outside, my twin sister went inside to get a drink of water. I thought she had been gone too long so I decided to find out what was going on. When I went inside the school building I found my twin sister with her head pressed down between the wall and the bench in an awkward position and her face almost blue. On top of her was a big nasty boy. Never mind my small stature, I was furious with that boy and I told him, "If you don't let go of my sister, I will let you have it!" He knew that I was not afraid of him, and I would put up a good fight, so he let go of her. By now the teacher had heard the commotion so she came out and took care of the boy. I was glad I didn't have to wrestle with him. It would have been an ugly fight for sure.

Since my father was a salesman and was tired of the farm, my parents sold it. We moved in with our paternal grandparents who lived in another village not too far from our former place. They had a very small house and we were eight people living there; my parents and our grandparents plus an uncle and we girls. It was located in a nice area with a forest behind the dwelling place, and a lovely garden of flowers in front of the home. There were lots of fine lilac bushes on the side of the homestead with their sweet fragrance filling the air, and in the middle stood a beautiful chestnut tree. Outside was plenty of space for us girls to play and have fun when we were free from schoolwork. My father, wanting to help his parents, had us help them stack the sheaves of oats, and as a reward for this we had the joy of riding in the hay wagon.

Later when my father's sisters and brothers and their families came for a visit, the whole house was filled with music and laughter. They all had either the gift of singing or playing instruments. Some of them were Christians, and I enjoyed the music very much.

We had many relatives but we got along with all of them really well, and we enjoyed being together with them. Also when our cousin Stig came for a visit we had a great time playing together. He was such a gentle boy, and always very kind to us girls. My uncle Hjalmar and his wife Elsa and Stig's younger sister Britt also visited us many times when we had moved to Vedum. We had many wonderful memories of them all. They lived in Gothenburg, the second largest city in Sweden, and they had to travel a little bit to see us, but we enjoyed being together so distance meant nothing. We were not together very often but when we saw each other we were all very happy, and there was a spread of wonderful food of all kinds.

Lured Into the Occult

It was at this time my father's brother Einar got me involved in the occult. He introduced me to levitation, and because of that, I also got into other things. I was just a child and had no knowledge of the danger in this; thus I opened up to evil powers.

My first school years had been very good, and I had fine grades, but after I got involved in the occult, things began to get bad. The teacher in the third grade made me terribly insecure. When he was angry, which happened quite frequently, he took a wooden stick and hit it as hard as he could on his desk. His face turned blood red, and it looked as though he was going to have a heart attack.

Unfortunately my grades went down, and I was given some extra homework because of one particular subject. My dad helped me, and I improved enough to finish the class.

Our New House

After my grandparents, Karl and Amanda Strom, died, my parents sold the little farmstead and bought a big Victorian house in Vedum. It was very sad watching my grandparents be so terribly sick before they died. Grandmother died of cancer, and grandfather of heart problems. I was wondering what happened to them after they died. Later I asked my dad what happens to people after they die. He answered that they would just go to sleep. My parents were not saved at that time, and I was a young girl, but I remember I was not satisfied with that answer but put it on the shelf for time being.

Their death made a strong impact on my life. I had liked them very much, and it was difficult to see them suffer so much, but I was thankful that they had accepted Jesus into their hearts, which was told me much later.

Now with this huge place, we girls were very happy to get our own room. Inside we had plenty of space, but outside there was just a very small garden. We had a nice fruit tree, some flowerbeds and bushes. My parents made it into a lovely, idyllic spot, where all of us could sit and relax from time to time. The house was located very close to a railroad track and would shake when the trains passed. It was a good thing during those years that not many trains passed. After awhile we got used to it, but I would always wake up to the sound of the trains.

On Mother's and Father's day, the three of us would get up early and make breakfast, putting it on a tray. Then we would surprise Dad and Mom with breakfast in bed. I loved my Dad, and when I got saved I forgave him everything. Although he was a very good provider, and I knew he cared for us, it became very clear to me that the only one that can give us unconditional love is our Heavenly Father. About six years before he got saved he confessed to my twin sister that he regretted deeply that he had been so hard on us. She was then married and she had two boys. Those boys became the joy of their lives, especially my father's life. The boy's names were Stefan, and Jorgen. My parents took care of those boys when my twin sister Daga and her husband Rolf had an engagement and they were not able to take them along with them. My older sister Vally, after she got married to Lennart, had two boys and their names were Ulf, and Thomas, and my parents took care of them also from time to time when my sister Vally and her husband needed their help.

When we were growing up I had to wear overalls most of the time, not-so-nice clothing, and very short hair. This caused me to look like a boy, but deep inside I was most feminine; I loved laces. When we started school we had better clothing, but it was not until I had grown up that I could buy the things that I really liked. Today I am thankful to God that I didn't have any toys; neither did we have any television to look at when I was growing up. There is nothing wrong with having toys, but I see so many parents go overboard.

I praise the Lord that my parents had honesty and integrity, and I never heard them argue. They always talked things over and then my dad made the decision. They never changed their minds after that. My mother was a very humble person and easy to love.

She was very gifted in weaving beautiful rugs, sewing embroidery, and she gave things to the Red Cross which they sold; they used the money for their organization to help people. Also she was a tremendous cook. She even used to work in a restaurant for awhile. We enjoyed her delicacies at home, and her baking was one of a kind. I was very observant and imitated most of the things she was doing, especially her baking, when I was in my young-teens. One time I surprised her with a spice cake with cranberries. That was my own creation, and it turned out very good and my mother liked it very much. For some reason she did not teach me very much, but when I showed interest and asked questions she was very willing to tell me more about baking.

She was very gifted, and she loved us all. As you read later in this story you will see how very close we became to them, my husband and I. As I mentioned earlier, my dad played the organ, but he also played banjo and mandolin. Mother seldom played the organ but when she did she read music, if I recall correctly. When I was alone I would listen to the songs they played on the radio, and later I would take my dad's mandolin and play those songs by ear. My sisters and I would sing pop songs together.

My uncle Einar, who got me interested in the occult, married a nice Christian lady. Through marrying her, he also came closer to Christ, and was now living for Him. If I recall correctly, he was a Christian before, but had not realized the danger of being involved in the occult. His wife's name was Elvira. Being a strong Christian, she had a great influence on his life, and he never got mixed up with the occult again. Our parents let them have a space on the third floor in our house until they could afford to buy their own home. She made a great impact on my life because of her kindness and love toward me, and she always took time to talk to me and listening to what I had to say.

My dad and his brother fixed up the first floor into a shoe and clog store. Dad made clogs as well as selling them all over the country. He was a very good businessman; he was excellent at figuring out the cost in his head. He was also very musically gifted. He was an excellent writer. He wrote the lyrics to the song which was sung at our wedding.

Going to Sunday School

It was during this time in my life that Elvira took me to Sunday school. This was the first time I went to a Baptist Church. I liked it very much, and I went there for quite some time. I learned many Christian songs, and can remember some of them to this very day. We were also taught the "Aftonbonen" (Evening Prayer). My twin sister and I would pray that prayer often, but I can't remember anyone ever explaining to us how to get saved, although we had begun to believe in God, as children will.

One day a guest preacher came to our church. She was so loud and aggressive that I thought she was angry with me, so I ran home. After a long time my aunt Elvira was able to get me back to the church again. This time they had a wonderful couple, Elly and Oliver, who had been missionaries to Brazil, and had came back to Sweden, to this church, to be teachers in the Sunday school. They told stories about that country which made a great impression on my heart. They taught us many songs and Bible stories, but before long they went back to the mission field. Needless to say, they left a very sad girl behind them. I had liked them a lot. Without realizing it, God had already begun to work in my heart.

In their place, a young man came that was also a good teacher and my twin sister went with me again. We looked up to him with respect. He taught us how to play a guitar, and we were having fun with the lessons. Things were looking up again. After some time had passed something embarrassing took place. One evening as he followed us out, while we were leaving to go home, he turned the outside light on and an unexpected thing happened — my underwear fell off! The underwear were way too big and ugly for me. I was so embarrassed that I took the underwear in a firm grip, put them in my coat pocket and acted like I was in a hurry, which I was, and I speedily went home. He never saw me again!

Elvira worked greatly to persuade me to go back to the church. However, I refused to go without ever telling her my reasons, nor did she ever ask. Sad to say, my pride wouldn't permit me to go back to that Baptist Church again.

Difficult School Years

After we moved to Vedum, we got a teacher who told us stories about his everyday life, but he taught us little.

When we entered the next grade, our new teacher was very angry because we had not learned what we were supposed to in the previous class, so he took it out on us. At that time I didn't understand why he was being so cruel and unfair, but later found out that he was using alcohol behind the scenes.

One time when I came to school riding on my bicycle, I met the teacher and tried my best to curtsy on the bike but he was not satisfied, so he made me curtsy in front of the whole class ten times. It was the custom, at that time, to curtsy to people who were older than you.

Later on we got an excellent educator and my grades went up immediately. Things were going fine for a while, but in my final school year I ended up with that nasty teacher again. Consequently I lost interest in schoolwork and just endured the class. Also, I was sick for some time, and got behind in the same subject which I had problems with earlier. But now it was more advanced, and I didn't dare tell my dad what was going on. I had lost much time when I was sick, and it was amazing that I even graduated.

After finishing school, it was required by the school district in Vedum that we take a course in home economics. Some girls we knew had taken this class before us, and they had warned us about the teacher we were going to have. They told us that some of the girls were having nightmares. She would intimidate us very often, and she had especially humiliated a girl that had problems with her hearing. She would degrade us and discipline us in strange ways. After awhile, the whole class decided to go on a strike. No one had ever dared to do this before, but I guess we had enough girls with the courage to do what it was going to take to see an end to what was going on in this class. So we did it. All of us got on our bicycles and took off to the next town where the principal was presiding. We told him exactly what had been going on in class. He was very nice and promised he was going to talk to her.

The next day she was very quiet, and she would only whisper what she wanted us to do; she didn't give us any more trouble so we were able to finish the course. During that time, in small places out in the country, it was not uncommon to have such an experience. In one way I felt sorry for her, she must have been a very unhappy person. There were a few teachers who were really good; they had moved out from the bigger cities because they wanted the fresh air and country living. There were other kinds of abuse during those years, but I forgave those people who were involved after I was saved and born again.

I had to attend some religious classes for the State Lutheran Church. I was bored to death, and saw it as unnecessary nonsense I had to go through. To memorize the catechism didn't help me any either. The Bible was a dead book to me at that time and the priest had no joy but looked more like a funeral director. To me everything about the church was depressing. I was very happy when I finally had my confirmation and it was all over. I was about 13-14 years old.

Chapter Two

My Teenage Years

Being Caught by the World

As a teenager I once tried to smoke, but after almost throwing up I promised myself never to touch another cigarette, and I never did. Alcohol had no attraction to me either. I had seen what it did to my Uncle Nils, and how it had affected his family, but later on in his life he gave up his drinking of alcohol.

One day he tried to kill himself by throwing himself before a train, but someone saw his intention and rescued him. There were other people I had seen who were completely intoxicated, and this made a horrible impression on me for life.

After this I got more and more involved in dancing, which I had taught myself and just loved. It was as if it was in my blood. During the summers of those years one of my best friends and I traveled by taxi to many different parks located all over the lovely forest. (In Sweden these parks were called "Folkparker," which means "the People's Parks. When Sweden was taken over by the Socialists in the early 1920's, they built a vast network of these parks in all communities. The purpose was to give people a place for amusement, but it also lured the young people away from the churches and made them worldly.)

We would dance to the orchestras we especially liked. One time it didn't turn out too well. We had gone to the park in our hometown, but there were just a few people there and it wasn't too good, so we decided to hitchhike to a park in another town. Two men were willing to take us to that place and as we had just gotten situated inside the car, suddenly another man showed up who also wanted to ride with us to the next park.

We had not planned on another man to showing up, but since we wanted to go dancing we decided not to say anything. When we had been traveling for a while, the guy who was sitting in the back seat with my friend Barbro and I tried to touch me. He most likely had some drinks before he entered into the car.

I got very upset and told the driver that I would jump out of the car if he didn't stop. When he saw that I had my hand on the door-handle he stopped the car. We were let out in the middle of a forest but I recognized where we were and knew there was a service station not too far away, so we walked there.

Our intention was to call home and have someone pick us up, but after a second thought, we decided that would be bad because our parents would be upset, so we choose to hitchhike home instead. By now we were extremely careful as we looked at the cars that were passing us. We saw a car with two men inside and we flagged them down. We checked them very carefully, asking them many questions. We found out that they were professional soccer players and they were known for their good reputations. They were very nice to us and said that they were going to take us back to our town since they were planning to go through Vedum anyhow on their way to their destination to play soccer. We could tell they knew we had a very bad experience, and they were very sensitive to us. They were true to their words and we arrived safely home; we thanked them and said good bye.

My Facination with Fiction Writing

I was immersed in reading detective storybooks. I thought a lot about becoming a private detective. One day I was so inspired, I wrote a detective story myself. In the evening, in dim light and with a dramatic voice, I read the story to my sisters. I had their full attention. I also had the ability to solve detective story mysteries and to know who was guilty at all times; but as time went on, I lost interest. However, Scotland Yard had an admirer in me. I also wrote some romantic stories that I shared with my sisters, to their delight. This I regretted because later they teased me about being romantic.

Teasing was something that I didn't care for and I wouldn't do it to other people. The last year in school a boy teased me quite often. He took the first letters of my first and last name to make a bad word, and thus he cursed me very often. I suffered much for that. Later on I found out the boy got polio when he became an adult.

In my teenage years I also had many pictures of movie stars hanging on the walls in my room. They became idols in my life. I went to a lot of movies, my favorites being American or British. There were only a few Swedish movies that I liked, but I did enjoy their comedies. I used to joke quite a bit, and after a movie I would imitate the actors. Many were the evenings when my sisters and I had gone upstairs to our room that I would have my comic acting in full swing. My sisters' roars of laughter would cause my dad to knock on the wall downstairs and we had to be quiet. But before I quit, I would manage, in a whispering voice, to tell some more stories from my imagination for my sisters' enjoyment.

As I mentioned earlier I became involved in the occult as a small child. Now I was reading horoscopes and predicting the future by using all kinds of items. I was also involved with ESP, and before I realized it, I had opened myself to all kinds of satanic oppression for which I paid a price. One price I paid was depression from time to time. Another was unexplained disease, which came and went in my body. I tried not to show this to my family. Since I had an easy-going personality, enjoyed being home on visits and was always happy during those occasions, they had no way of telling what was going on inside of me. I kept my physical body in good shape by cross-country skiing, bicycling and all the dancing I did.

Starting to Work

When I finished school, I worked close to my hometown for several years. I took the train to my job every day working as a domestic aide, but in reality I was more like a nanny. I took total care of a young child and did all the shopping, cooking, baking, etc. Sometimes I would assist with the patients since the woman I was working for was a masseuse.

Later on, Barbro and I began our first work together at a nursing home at the same place. That took some time to get used to, but there were great rewards in that field. This town was closer to my parents' place and every second weekend I took the bus and paid them a visit.

In time my friend and I quit the job at the nursing home. There were things going on that were not right, and it was very depressing. I shared this with my dad, and he wholeheartedly agreed it was time to look for another job. One day dad saw a good paying job advertised in the paper and informed me about it. This job was located in a city further away from my hometown. Dad encouraged me by offering to drive me to the city; so I decided to go for it. Going to a big city was a new adventure. The administrator interviewed me, and hired me on the spot. The best part of it all was that I got my own apartment, which was free along with all the other benefits. Also included were three free meals a day. Both dad and I were very happy I got this job.

This was a big rest home, and I was able to bring happiness to the patients. I had experience from my former job, and I felt I could bring joy to those older people and make their days brighter. I looked forward to getting to know them. The name of the city was Trollhattan, a beautiful city with its gorgeous canal and small idyllic island in the midst of it. I really had begun to like it and since I had more money to spend, I could afford to go out to fancy restaurants, dance to excellent orchestras, buy the best clothing and still have money left over. Every second weekend I was free, but since Trollhattan was located further away from my hometown I had to take the train when I went back to visit my parents. I didn't have a car during those years in Sweden. They had very fine inexpensive transportation.

If it had not been for my involvement in dancing, which I loved so much, I would have probably been more home sick, but that plus my demanding job kept me very busy. I didn't mind because I had been used to working, even temporary work, since I was in grammar school. When we had free time from school, each one of us girls had to go to different relatives who had farms, and we would help pick berries and do other chores. Although they were very nice, and I didn't mind the work itself, it was just not home.

A Miracle

After I had worked for some time, I had an unusual experience on my job. The lady who cleaned the windows in that big retirement place got sick. The boss came to me and another lady, and asked us if we would like to help out with the windows. We said we would be happy to do this. Those were huge windows, and we had to open them up to clean them from inside. Suddenly I lost the window and it fell down. The other lady screamed, "Aina, now you have to pay for that window!" It most likely was very expensive. The glass lay in thousands of pieces. We were working on the second floor, and on the ground there was lots of gravel. That is where the window landed. I didn't wait for the elevator, but I ran down the stairs. Just as I was going out from the building to the place were the gravel was, I met the maintenance man and he gave me a smile and he said, "Aina, you have a guardian angel." I had no clue why he said that, but when I came to the place where the window was laying and I took a good look at it, I could not believe what I saw. The glass was not broken, and there was not a scratch on the frame either. Later, when I became a born again Christian, God brought to my mind what really had happened that day. My soapy hands caused the window to slip out of my hands and fall to the gravel below. However, it was brought to my attention that the window did not fall according to the law of gravity, but it was like someone had taken hold of it just in time. I had been too concerned about the window to think about that at that time, but it was later revealed to me that God had used His angel to take care of that window.

Soaring Like an Eagle

In Trollhattan, I became friends with a lady by the name of Ann Britt, who became my best friend. One time I had the privilege of flying with her boyfriend Rune and a friend of his, who owned a small airplane. I had the joy of seeing the beautiful city of Trollhattan from the air in a small 3-seat Cessna type airplane. Ann Britt was waiting on the ground at that time.

Trying to Learn English

Prior to getting the job in Trollhattan there weren't any courses to improve grades if one had gotten a bad grade in one subject. Besides that, I didn't have high self-esteem. Later on, there were courses offered to help, but by that time I already had my good paying job. With the bad memories about teachers and schools, I was not very interested in more schooling.

Nevertheless, when my close friend Ann Britt asked me to join her in taking an English class, I enrolled. We had barely begun when we both became very ill with the Asian flu, so the teacher told me I had lost too much time to catch up and I would have to get back to class some time in the future. One day I saw an advertisement in the paper for an English course by mail; one could study at one's own speed at home. I thought this sounded great, so I signed up for the program

One day, to my surprise, I got a phone call from the study program representative who was in the area and wanted to see me. I didn't feel too good about that, but wanted to find out what it was all about, so I invited a friend to be with me. She was working in the same place and had an apartment beneath me. The representative went through the lesson with us but he didn't seem to care too much if we got hold of it or not. I was again very disappointed, and had really had it with all education as far as I was concerned.

During this time in my life I had an appendectomy. While in the hospital, I had a dream in which I asked the doctor in English, "Do you speak English?" He answered me, "No," and then I woke up. It seems like English was getting into my mind; circumstances didn't let me have any success in this, but I was not going to be let down by it. Maybe something later on would work out for me.

Chapter Three

Getting Married

Meeting My Husband to Be

At this time I had been dating a few men but I hadn't found anyone I thought I'd like to marry. Usually we would have a cup of coffee with some rolls and cookies, and just spend the time talking. Most of those men were very snobbish and had great egos. Because of that I lost interest very soon, even if they were good dancers.

I had worked in Trollhattan about two years and had just visited my parents in Vedum and was on my way back to the city. In the afternoon I boarded the train and got a nice seat close to a window so that I could enjoy seeing the familiar sight of the farmlands, the groves of trees and the beautiful meadows that came into view. Down deep in my heart I was still that same shy person I had always been. The big city life had not changed me at all in that respect.

I sat in the train in my compartment reading my favorite magazine. I looked up for a moment and noticed two gentlemen who were staring intensely at me. I just continued to read my weekly periodical. Suddenly, both of them entered into the compartment where I was sitting. They passed me and were slowly walking into the next section, which was a smoking compartment. Soon they came back and asked if they could sit down and talk with me. I was on my guard, but I said yes. They introduced themselves and gave their names and the city they were coming from. Since they were sitting opposite me I noticed that John was very handsome. We were involved in a pleasant conversation and John inquired of me where I was coming from and where I was going. Thus we found out that we were all going to the same city. I also learned where he came from and that he was studying to become an engineer in the same city where I worked. He appeared to me to be very serious and sincere.

When we arrived in the town of Vara the train broke down and was not able to take us to our destination. At the railroad station they told us to take a bus instead. John and his friend asked me if I knew the different connections we had to make to get us where we were going. It was my pleasure to inform them that I had taken that route before so I knew the area quite well. We boarded the bus and took off. I had taken many train rides in my life but never had an engine in a locomotive broken down before. John's friend, Svenningson, became very interested when he found out that my older sister Vally was working temporarily at the same place as I was; he wanted us all to go out together, which we later did.

Our Wedding

John and I continued our dating and we became very fond of each other. He was a person that I could talk to about anything. Later on, we became engaged and waited about a year before we got married. Before we were engaged I had met his parents, and to my relief they liked me right away. My parents liked John as well. I had also met Reinert, and he became like a brother to me that I never had. On my job I took care of a patient who had a son who was a priest. He came often to visit his mother so I got to know him very well. He was very nice to me, so with John's approval, we decided to have him marry us. His name was Ake Johansson

We had a beautiful wedding. The ceremony took place in a small country Lutheran Church. I asked to have the choir sing, and also the coming in and going out music. My father surprised me with a man who played a violin solo, *The Sater Girl's Sunday.* This song tells about a country girl's Sunday far up in the northern part of Sweden. I wore a real gold tiara with expensive pearls and a Spanish veil. Those I had rented; they were too costly to buy. My parents paid for my long white dress with laces of flowers. I bought my shoes and my wedding flowers, golden soft yellow roses and white daisies. My best friend Ann Britt and my sister Vally were the maids of honor. My husband's best friends Reinert, and Rune were his best men. Lena, John's cousin, was the flower girl at the wedding ceremony. My father, mother, my brother-in-law Rolf, my twin sister Daga, and other relatives and friends were present. My friend Barbro was also there. One of the songs the choir sang had the same melody as *Fairest Lord Jesus.* I still had not accepted Jesus as my personal Savior, but I was deeply touched by those songs.

Before the wedding I had the most relaxed time in my life with the hairdressers fixing my hair and taking care of my face; then, finally, they put the tiara on my head and the veil. I looked like a princess, but I was really a joyful bride. After this preparation, John and I went to the studio and had our pictures taken. After this we traveled to the church, which was located outside the city in the countryside. Some of the pictures which had been taken at the wedding were taken by a school friend of John's, whose name was Karl Gustav. Reinert also took some pictures at that time.

I had made the arrangement for all of us to travel to a city not too far from Trollhattan. That city's name was Vanersborg, and its nickname was Little Paris. There we had the wedding dinner. The soft pink sweet peas I had arranged spread a sweet aroma all over the room. The people at the restaurant had put a beautiful candleholder with fine candles at the head table and my wedding flowers in the middle. Later my cousin Arne played accordion and Allen who played the violin at the church also played the piano at the dinner. There were some games and the telegrams were read, and everyone had brought beautiful gifts to us. My father paid for the great dinner that we all enjoyed. We were also happy that Arne's girlfriend Anna-Greta was able to be there. Our wedding took place in the autumn, when the leaves on the trees were in their most gorgeous colors. This might be difficult to believe, but I arranged the whole wedding alone.

We had decided we were not going to have any alcohol or dancing at our wedding, so that we each gave up something. Earlier John had told me that he almost died from being too intoxicated with alcohol. John also told me he used to be a gang leader, had a nightclub, and had, at one time, been in a gang fight. To defend himself, he used a knife and cut his opponent very badly. But his life was spared, and so was John's. This was very significant that both their lives were spared. If that man had died, my husband would not have been able to come to America, and I would not have been his wife. A chain of events in our lives, and in the lives of many others, would never have occurred: our meeting with Jesus Christ as Savior and Lord, John's call to be a preacher of the gospel, my call to be his partner in this ministry, and the touch of the Holy Spirit and miracles in the lives of people that we ministered to. We will always be thankful for the faithful preachers of this beautiful country that gave us the full gospel. For myself, first came MY JOURNEY TO FREEDOM, then MY JOURNEY OF FAITH.

Moving to Jonkoping

I couldn't help but recall a time earlier in my life when I used to fantasize that I should marry and help someone that ended up on the wrong side of the law. This was during the time I was reading all the detective stories and wanted to become a private detective. With this marriage, I realized that this is exactly what had happened.

The nice nurse who worked with me on my job quit. The person who took her place acted like she was the boss. It looked to me like the real supervisor was afraid of her. This made it very difficult for me since they both wanted me at the same time. The stress of that job caused me to get very sick so we decided to move to John's hometown and live there instead. Another reason for us to move was John had failed some subjects. This failure had a lot to do with what had happened earlier in his life. After I got some rest and recuperated, we moved.

John's mother Maj-Britt had good connections, since she was working as a secretary in the Husqvarna Factory. Her boss was Dr. Bertil Tyberg who was a foundry engineer; he had friends high-up in the State Board Of Education. Because of that help, John's mother was able to get John into the college in Jonkoping.

It wasn't long before I got a nice job in a Christian retirement center. It was a very nice atmosphere to work in. While there, I was searching for God. I think the reason was that the Holy Spirit had begun to work in my life. One time they invited me to go to a conference and I had hoped that someone would explain to me how to get to know Jesus, but no one ever did. I was very disappointed over this. The same situation existed at my job. I can't recall any time that anyone ever told me how to have a personal relationship with Jesus Christ.

Chapter Four

Moving to the United States

Our Journey to the United States

At the time we were engaged, John had talked a lot about going to The United States of America. I thought it might be another fad he would lose interest in after awhile, but after some time he was still talking about it. It was then I realized he was very serious in this matter. I was a very adventurous type. So I thought this would be great, especially since he told me that we would only stay for two years and then we would be moving to Germany. The reason was that he was planning to join the army in America, and then ask for a transfer to Germany.

My parents and John's father Sture were not happy at all about this, but his mother thought it was a great idea. Father tried very hard to talk us out of going. My sisters couldn't believe that I was planning to leave, and it was hard for them to grasp hold of it. Mother made me promise to be back in two years, according to our plan. It would be difficult to be separated from my family, but I told myself, since it was only to be for a short time, I should be able to manage it. I had always wanted to see other countries, so to be able to take a closer look at this big country of America would be just great.

Finally, the day for John's graduation came, and some of our families came to celebrate this occasion. I was very happy to have been of help in getting John through college by working and supporting us.

It was just a few days before we were to leave Sweden and I was happy I had a part in John's graduation. Earlier, some well-meaning people had encouraged me to get into the restaurant business, or marry a farmer who was well-off, but my dream was to be a designer. Therefore, I enjoyed drawing an engine for John's graduation project. From time to time, he had let me examine his homework. Now a new adventure was waiting for us.

The last night before we were to leave Sweden, John began to have doubts about our going. We'd already had the farewell party, and all of our friends and my twin sister Daga and her husband Rolf plus relatives had given us gifts. I couldn't see myself giving them back and telling them we had changed our minds. Not only was I a proud person, but also I would never waiver once my mind was made up. We discussed it for a while and then he agreed we should do as we had planned.

My parents, my older sister, John's parents, his brother Peter and our best friend Reinert bid us farewell at the airport. It was difficult but we looked forward to the end of the two years, which would go very fast. The year was 1963 when we left Sweden.

40

Arriving in Salt Lake City

Earlier we had made all the arrangements with John's uncle and family who were sponsoring us, to meet us at the airport in Salt Lake City. They had been living there for a long time. The trip went fine. When we finally landed, a lot of John's relatives were there to greet us. I was completely overwhelmed since I had only met John's uncle and didn't know anyone else. They separated us so I went in one car and my husband in another. As we drove through the city, I felt a terrible depression and darkness, and I didn't know what to make of that.

We were exhausted after such a long journey. The time change had also done something to us, but they insisted on having a party for us that evening with all of John's relatives. It was not easy to come to a strange country and meet people I didn't know, but I was doing my best under the circumstances.

John's uncle had arranged for John to work as a bricklayer. They felt he should have the same experience as they had when they first came to this country, so they refused to help him get a better job even though they knew he had graduated as an engineer. Where he was working was extremely hot and dirty, and when he came home he took a bath, had his dinner and went to bed; this continued for some time. This was a sad time for us because John came home totally exhausted so was too tired to talk with me. I felt very lonely, and missed the wonderful communication we had always had. Since I spoke no English and understood very little, I just had to endure it.

Our First Apartment

After we had stayed with family for a while, we had a conflict so we

41

moved out. They were Mormons and really wanted us to join their church. I had a strong feeling not to get involved with their church so John wouldn't join either. We had nothing against them as people, and we were thankful that John's uncle had sponsored us to be able to move to this country, but now it was time for us to get our own place. We didn't have much money left, but I had seen an apartment for rent in the paper that would fit our budget; we went there, talked to the landlord, and we got the place. The apartment was on the second floor of an old house in a slum area. It was not easy for us to live there since we had come from such a high standard, but we had each other, and we were determined to make a go of it. In these living quarters we had very old and not so clean furniture, and plastic curtains for the windows.

One day, when it was very hot, the room began to spin. In the window was an old beat-up air conditioner that didn't work as it should, and one day when it was extra hot the whole room began to spin to me. The last thought that came to my mind was, 'I must somehow get to my bed.' The next thing I knew I was laying on the top of the bed, not feeling good at all. Before long the doorbell rang and I managed to go and open the door; outside the doorway, stood one of John's cousins. When she realized what had happened to me, she told me to go with her to her mother's place to cool off until John came back from work. I was grateful she had come to pick me up, and I recovered fairly quickly. When John came back from his job we bought some salt tablets, which someone had recommended to us. We also fixed up the air conditioner and that helped somewhat, but coming from a northern climate, we still had a difficult time getting used to the heat. When we first arrived in this country I had problems with my lungs and John had nose bleeds, but this went away as we became more accustomed to the area.

I wanted to get a job, so John gave me a crash course in English, and I managed to get employment at the Ramada Inn Hotel. John had written up some possible things I might encounter in my work, but there were lots more unexpected things that came up during my time there. Somehow I was able to manage, using my hands a lot. Not very long after this, a fruit company employed me. I began to pick up more English, but this was just a seasonal job so it was soon over.

Later on we were able to get one of John's cousins to take him to the Highway Department for a job interview. Seeing his diploma as an engineer, they were amazed to learn what kind of work he had been doing. They hired him and trained him in his job as a Design Engineer. This was in the Right-of-Way Division.

I was able to get a very nice job in a big department store working as a sales lady. Earlier, I had taken some classes in English for foreign born people. This went very well, and I was thrilled over the wonderful teachers they gave me. It was not long before I was enrolled in Adult Education. I had felt all along that someone was really helping me, and somehow I knew it must have been God. What a joy it was for me to have so many outstanding teachers to help me in my education.

In 1965 we had moved to a very fine apartment. It was then that John and I began to listen to a Christian radio program called "The Hour of Decision" with Billy Graham as the speaker. John had brought our Swedish Bibles with us. Two years had gone by and I had experienced a variety of feelings and experiences during that time, but the worst thing I had to cope with was homesickness. It was very difficult during the holidays. Besides that, I had a headache every day.

Galleria

Aina, Vally and Daga

Aina and Daga

Daga, Vally, and Aina

Aina

Daga

L to R 1st row: Daga #3 and
Aina #4 second grade

L to R: Aunt Helga, Grandfather Karl, Uncle
Hjalmar, grandmother Amanda,
and my Dad

Picture of my grandparents' home

Standing, fifth from the left is Daga and
I am sitting in front of her
in our class at age 13.

L to R: Daga and Aina
as teenagers.

L to R: Vally, Aina and
our friend Gudrun.

L to R: Daga and Aina

My parents, Helge and Valborg Strom

Our house in Vedum.

Our engagement picture 1st row, L to R:
John, Aina, Vally, Daga and her husband Rolf,
2nd row, L to R: Mother and Father.

Cousin Stig Strom

L to R: Uncle Einar Strom, his wife Elvira
and daughter Margareta in their home.

John's parents, Sture and Maj-Britt
Thorell

Our wedding picture

47

The state Lutheran church building
we were married in.

John's graduation from college, with
Aina in front of his parents' house

Farewell party for John and Aina
before going to America

More guests at farewell party

John and Aina on the day of departure for
America with their four suitcases standing in
front of John's parents' house

The airplane we flew on to Salt Lake
City in 1963

Central Baptist Church in Salt
Lake City, our first church home

Our 1st Pastor, Robert McCullar, his wife
Gween and their children
Stanley and Carla.

Our 2nd Pastor, James McFatridge, his wife
Linda and their children Richard,
Kathy and Phyllis

Aina on the way to a revival meeting,
standing at the seminary in front of the
building we lived in.

John and the revival team from the
seminary that John and Aina
traveled with in California.

Aina during our time at the seminary.

49

John preaching at a tent meeting in Sweden

Our van and trailer in front of revival tents in 1973 in Sweden

John baptizing in a lake in Sweden

People watching the baptism at the lake

Pastor Tord Krigsstrom ready to baptize in his church

Pastor Tord is baptizing the man that was taken as a young boy from Denmark by the Nazis and trained as a Satan worshipper in Germany.

John and Aina at the 1974 Crusade
Meetings in Vara, Sweden

John and Aina with the entire 1974
crusade team in Vara

Aina took the picture of
John and her cousin Arne Strom
and his wife Anna-Greta in 1974

L to R: Carl and Gota Ahman, Aina,
Pastor Krigsstrom and team singers at
an open air meeting in Sweden

L to R: Owen Bergh, Ben Hanegraaf, Dutch
evangelist and Aina walking in Holland

L to R: John, Aina, Marion and Wid Coryell
at a crusade meeting in Sweden, 1979

51

John and Aina standing in front of the
ferry that took them from
Sweden to Finland

Thorell family in 1979: 1st row L to R:
Maj-Britt, our niece Rachelle, Sture.
2nd row L to R: Monica, Peter, our
nephew Charles, John and Aina

Our nephew Joshua Thorell, born in 1987

L to R: Rolf, Daga, Aina and John on
their visit to Lake Tahoe, CA in 1987

Vally and husband Lennart celebrating her
60th birthday in Carmel, CA
visiting John and Aina

John's best friend from high school
Reinert Sollfors and his wife Maj-Britt at
their wedding in Sweden

Chapter Five

Being Born Again

Our Meeting With God

Now my English had improved and I was able to understand the language much better. In the beginning John translated the evangelist's sermons and I checked out the different Bible verses he used in my Swedish Bible to see if they were the same. God had now begun to open me up to His word, and one day they advertised that they were going to have a crusade on television.

I shall never forget that evening in the month of May, 1965 as we sat in our living room to watch this program on TV. What a beautiful sight it was to see and hear the big choir and to hear all those voices singing for the glory of God. I was deeply touched by the song leader Cliff Barrows, who seemed to move every inch of his body with the music. The music and the man were united together in complete harmony, and the whole stadium was filled with all kinds of people. The atmosphere was absolutely electrifying. The Holy Spirit was preparing those hearts, as well as the ones in the television audience.

After the music had finished, Billy Graham preached a sermon, and then he gave an invitation and asked the people to come forward to the platform, which had become the altar. Suddenly the people were streaming to the altar. They came in masses, and when we saw this we realized what we had to do. The Holy Spirit had opened our hearts to understand the full depth of the gospel. They had a close-up picture of the evangelist as the choir sang softly in the background and he spoke to the TV audience. He said, "If you are sitting in your living room, or in a bar, or wherever you may be, you can accept Jesus Christ right where you are." As I looked at his eyes I didn't see the man anymore but I saw God's eyes looking at me with such a burning love and compassion that I had no doubt that this was the Lord speaking to me.

During this time John and I had not spoken a word to each other. The power of the Holy Spirit was so strong that no words were uttered but we both silently repented of our sins and asked Jesus to come into our hearts. When we did this, we really became twins in Christ. Now I had a *spiritual* twin as well as a physical twin

Later on, as I was lying in my bed praying to God and communicating with Him about my difficulty to forgive myself, I had an unusual experience. I felt like I was utterly weightless, and I was floating above my bed. First I was afraid, and I wondered what was happening to me; when I got frightened I was back in my bed again. I continued to pray to God, and the same thing happened twice, but by now my fear was completely gone and it was a beautiful feeling. Jesus gave me such peace and there was an overwhelming love that was engulfing me. If the ceiling had fallen down on me it would not have had any affect on me at all. I did not realize that it was God's Holy Spirit that had lifted me up and I was totally filled with His sweet agape love. Later I found out that it is called the Baptism of the Holy Spirit. John had gone to sleep, but I woke him up and excitedly told him what had happened to me. He was happy that I had such an encounter with God although he had not had the same thing happen to him. Then we both went to sleep.

When I woke up the next morning I felt like the whole world was smiling at me. Everything was different. I was a new creature in Christ, full of joy and love. My life had changed totally, and would never be the same again. This took place in May, 1965

With this love burning in our hearts we just couldn't keep it for ourselves. We wanted to especially share this good news with our families and relatives. Earlier we had purchased a tape recorder, so we shared with them how we had accepted Jesus into our lives, and we also asked them for forgiveness for anything we might have done wrong to them in the past. I gave a message in song and then we sent the tape to them. We got a very good response to that tape. My sisters commented about my singing, and mentioned how my voice had changed compared to earlier in our youth.

They were amazed and I was glad to tell them that it was the anointing that made the difference in my voice.

During this time I kept trying to get my husband to go to a church with me, but since he was uncertain which one was the right one, he wouldn't go at all. I didn't want to go alone so neither of us went, but we continued to listen to our regular Christian program on the radio every Sunday.

A Trip Back to Sweden

Several months earlier I had become quite ill with an unusual virus, so I was not working at that time. I was in much pain. To walk and move my arms was pure agony. This virus was located behind the wall of the heart, but it was really in the lung. The doctor didn't give me much encouragement since he told me that it could take up to 10 years before the infection would be gone. There was really no cure for it, but he recommended a change in climate, so we decided that I should go back to Sweden for a visit. At that time we couldn't afford to make the trip together so I was to fly alone. The year was 1965 and it was toward the end of July. John and his supervisor Bill Plumhof took me to the airport. I was sad to leave my husband behind, but if this trip would get me well again it would be worth the price.

The flight went fine and my parents picked me up at the airport and gave me a great welcome. It was wonderful to see my loved ones after two years of absence.

My mother had ordered a cake especially for me and had written "Welcome Home Aina" on it. The whole town knew I had come home. I don't think that a celebrity would have had any better treatment. My older sister came with a beautiful bouquet of yellow roses and blue cornflowers to welcome me home. My twin sister and family came with gorgeous flowers as well, to show how happy they were that I was home again. It was lovely to see them all again. Later my older sister said, "I am sure glad that you have not forgotten your Swedish!" All my relatives wanted to see me, so I went to many gatherings but I also rested a lot and I began to feel much better.

My parents had invited some of the relatives who lived close to where my parents had their home. They all wanted to see me before my trip back to the USA. My Mother had prepared a wonderful dinner, and my cousin Arne and his wife Anna-Greta, and his brother Kurt and his wife Margareta came. This was the first time I met her, but she was so easy to talk to that I almost felt that I had known her all my life. Before this time I had met Kurt briefly, and he complimented me about the beautiful gestures I had with my hands. I then told him I used my hands a lot in my communication with the people in the USA since I did not speak English when I first came there. I was also happy to see my Uncle Einar and Elvira and we all had a great time. After dinner I showed slides of John and I and the places we had seen in America, and they truly enjoyed those.

During this time volumes of love letters were going back and forth over the Atlantic Ocean. With the times of happiness were also the times of sadness because I missed my husband very much. John was keeping himself very busy during my time away from him. He had begun to work as a painter in addition to his engineering job.

On another continent, my dad and I had made an appointment to see a doctor in Ekeberg's Sanatorium. While I was waiting for the doctor to talk to me, my thoughts were on my dad who was outside taking a walk around the place while he waited for me. I knew he was anxious about the outcome. His sister had most likely been in this place when she had tuberculosis many years earlier and then died of that disease.

The doctor came back after having gone through the x-rays and told me that I was free from the virus disease — there were no signs of it. It was all gone! What a relief it was to hear that good news. My dad was very happy too.

I became aware that I had changed a lot since I turned my life over to God. The things that I used to love, I didn't care for anymore. What a thrill to be able to tell my aunt Elvira face to face what had happened to me. As she heard my story she began to cry tears of joy and she hugged me and told me, "If you only knew how happy I am over this!" My firm belief is it was her prayers which kept me from getting involved with false religions and thus, she was the instrument God used to get me saved.

Saved From an Airplane Crash

John had arranged my trip back to the United States, and the tickets were already purchased, when one day a still small voice spoke to me that this wasn't the right time to go. Although I was only a baby Christian, I believed that the voice I had heard was Jesus speaking through the Holy Spirit. I contacted my husband immediately and used the excuse that my twin sister was making a dress for me and she wanted to have me try it on one more time. She lived in another area and I was staying with my parents at the time. This was the truth; she wanted to be sure the dress would fit me perfectly, so my husband agreed that we could change the plan and I would come back a few days later.

While I was gone overseas, I had a feeling that John was not doing very well with his walk with God, although he had not written much about it. In fact, he had begun to backslide and had taken up his beer drinking again.

I shall never forget my return flight. My uncle in Gothenburg took me to the airport. My flight was scheduled for early in the morning, but it was November and snowing hard. I could not leave until the weather cleared up in the middle of the day. Because of that, I lost my direct flight to New York and was booked with another flight on a different plane going to Frankfurt, Germany. When I arrived there I found out that I had missed my flight to New York, so the airlines arranged for me to stay at the airport hotel in Frankfurt with a free dinner. Since my airplane was not taking off until early in the morning, I decided to take advantage of my free meal, so I went to the restaurant where I had some very good food; because I was so happy, I gave the waiters very big tips.

The next day, as I was leaving, a large group of waiters stood in front of me and said something in German, but unfortunately I was not able to understand them. So I said, "Auf Wiedersehen," and the men gave me a big smile and everybody in chorus said the same thing; then I left. Well, I had asked for it. I had given them the impression that I was a very rich lady, which I was not.

My flight went well and my husband picked me up at the airport in Salt Lake City. Guess who was happy to see each other that day! It had been a long separation, but we were thankful I had been completely healed of the virus lung disease.

Later, John told me what had happened to the airplane that I should have taken. It had crash-landed at Salt Lake City airport. Many had died and some were much burned. This shook my husband up a lot and he realized that God had spared my life. It brought him back to a right relationship with Jesus. I was deeply touched, and very grateful that I had been obedient to the voice of Jesus, and was moved by His love for me.

Finding a Church

We still had not found a church where we wanted to attend. Then one day I saw in the newspaper that they were going to show a Christian movie at one of the movie houses. We decided to see it. We thought perhaps there would be someone at that place we could talk to about churches, so we went.

Sure enough, after the movie was over there was an invitation to come forward. In our case it was to publicly acknowledge that we had accepted Jesus Christ as Savior in our lives. As we were waiting for someone to talk to us (there was a big line of people in front of us) we noticed a man kept passing by us over and over, and then he finally stopped and came over and talked to us. He said, "I am an advisor and I am not really supposed to talk with you because this is the job of the counselors, but I feel very strongly that the Holy Spirit has led me to converse with you."

We told him our story and had a beautiful conversation with him. We found out he was the pastor for the Central Baptist Church, which was located in the downtown area. His name was Robert McCullar, and he invited us to his church. We went there for the Sunday morning service and enjoyed it very much. The week before the first time we went to church, almost the whole congregation visited us in our home. The first evening Pastor Robert and his wife Gwen came, the next evening deacon Ron Purvis with his wife Carol came, and the night after that a small delegation from the church visited us. We were overwhelmed with the love that they showed us, and decided this was the right church for us.

Soon we were baptized in water and also became members. We went to every meeting they had, and after some time we became Sunday school teachers and were involved in their visitation program, plus other things. We were both working, and in the evening I attended Adult Education School and that kept us very busy.

Chapter Six

Testing of My Faith in God

In My Loneliest Hours, Jesus Let Me Know I Was His Own

While John and I were still in Salt Lake City, there were a couple of incidents which tested us to the core, and also showed us the mighty power of God and His closeness to His children.

One day my husband became very ill with a throat infection and a raging fever. I called our doctor, and he told me to take him straight to a hospital where he would join us. A friend from our church came to help me get John into the car and drove us to the hospital. When we arrived at the hospital John was put into a wheelchair, and a nurse took him in an elevator to bring him to a room designated just for him. I was able to go with John to this room and as I stood there waiting for the doctor, John asked me to put his socks on his feet. This request surprised me because he always had warm feet. John was chilled despite the fever, and I realized that he was extremely sick. My heart ached as I was impacted with the seriousness of his illness. Then the nurse looked at me with ice-cold eyes. Another woman working at the hospital gave my husband a foot-massage. I felt bad not to be able to stay at my husband's side at this critical condition, but since I was not encouraged to stay; I went back to our apartment.

Just thinking of my husband lying in a hospital bed, deathly ill, and surrounded by total strangers was devastating to me. To make matters worse, one of the hospital staff left me with a bad impression. I had to go to bed that night, but as I lay there in my bed I began to pray, and as I prayed a beautiful peace came over me and I felt my faith rise again. I would not believe my husband was going to die in that hospital and God gave me faith that he would be healed. God answered my prayer and John was restored to perfect health in a very short time.

My Battle With the Headache

I had been having severe headaches every day and although I had been to several doctors, they each had a different diagnosis. One thought it was a migraine; another, nervous tension; and still another, a sinus infection. The wife of a couple in our church with whom we had become fairly well acquainted was a lab technician in a hospital. So I made an appointment to see a doctor there. As I spoke with this doctor, he said that he wanted to rule out a tumor on the brain, so he wanted to check my brain waves as soon as possible. I was immediately placed in a small room on a bed and hooked up to electrodes. There was a small window through which I could see technicians monitoring me from another room. As I lay there with all the wires connected to my head, I felt led to pray for God's protection.

64

Suddenly, without any warning, a terrible thing happened! I was given an electric shock! There was a very bright light, and I had an awful feeling that my eyes were open, but I knew they were closed. Since I was all wired up and helpless, all could do was to moan and groan, "NO, NO."

Finally they stopped shooting electrical impulses through my brain, and the technician came into the room and removed all of the wires. Tears were rolling down my cheeks and I was speechless. The technician commented, "Look how you are messing up your face." He was a man without compassion. I cleaned my face and left there in a big hurry to see my friend who worked in another section of the hospital

When I told Myrtle Stunnel what had happened to me, she exclaimed, "That doctor is experimenting on you, and if I were you I wouldn't go back to him." Of course, I had no intention of going back to him.

This was not a regular hospital, but a medical research center. Before I left, my friend told me to open the freezer. When I opened the door, a big monkey was staring at me. The monkey had been killed and frozen. This did not make me feel any more comfortable. When I returned home, I told my husband all that had transpired. Instead of being helped by that doctor, I was totally crushed, but God is faithful, and never left me for a moment.

Healed From My Headache

It was after we moved to Sacramento, California, that God once and for all healed me of the headaches that had plagued me for so many years. We attended a meeting in the San Francisco Bay Area to hear an evangelist whose name is Bill Basansky who had the gift of knowledge. When I went forward for prayer, he confirmed to me that the cause of the headaches was an infection of my sinuses. He prayed for me and I had to fight the enemy for two months before I was healed completely. The headaches have never come back.

Surely he hath borne our griefs, and carried our sorrows: yet we did esteem him stricken, smitten of God, and afflicted. But he was wounded for our transgressions; he was bruised for our iniquities: the chastisement of our peace was upon him; and with his stripes we are healed.
(Isaiah 53:4-5)

Moving to American Fork

Later on we had some incidents which tested us to the limits, and they also showed us the mighty power of God and His closeness to His children, as we trust Him with our lives every day. After some time had passed, my husband was transferred to a position in the Highway Department in American Fork, Utah, and we moved down to this place.

During this time we were still traveling back to Salt Lake City every Sunday. The place where we rented our house was in an area where there were few neighbors. Most of them were going to the Mormon Church, which had a doctrine we didn't agree with. We loved those people anyhow, and we were praying that one day they also would know the true gospel.

It was a very difficult time for us. My husband was working, and had our only car; I had no job except taking care of the house. To make matters worse, the headache I had before had also intensified.

One day to our joy, we received a tape from my uncle Hjalmar Strom in Gothenburg, in Sweden. On that tape he had recorded a man who was a former opera singer, Jan Sparring, who recently had become a Christian. My uncle recorded his personal testimony live at a restaurant in that area. We were both very touched as we heard him speak and sing. This is what God was using to make my husband see that he was called into full time ministry.

Back to Salt Lake City

We had lived in American Fork, Utah, for about six months when we found out there was a job opening for John in another district with the Highway Department in Salt Lake City. He was transferred with an increase of pay, and I got a job in a department store.

In the spring of 1967, my husband and I began a tape ministry to our families in Sweden. To our joy my cousin Arne and his wife Anna-Greta, plus their children, accepted Christ into their hearts in 1969. Later my father and mother accepted the Lord in 1970. Oh how happy we were over this wonderful news that also they had taken that final step.

Healed From Going Blind

Sometime later in 1968, I found out that I had gotten another virus. This time it was located in my eyes. I was working at a K-MART store as a sales lady. One day my left eye looked horrible and my co-workers could not stand to look at me. The boss was kind enough to give me the rest of the day off, and John and I went to an eye doctor. After he had examined my eyes he took my husband aside and told him that this virus was incurable, so it was no use to do any surgery on the eyes. I had a feeling it was bad news and I talked to my husband and he told me everything. This was a big blow to us. I thought about being blind, and not being able to see God's beautiful creation and the people that I loved. Before long my right eye became blurry.

Every morning my eyes were closed and I had to open them with some liquid. My regular doctor had to leave, and he had another eye doctor help me during his absence. I was sitting in the waiting room when I overheard the conversation the two doctors had about my eyes. The new doctor asked my regular doctor if he could use a special medication for my eyes that he wanted to try out on me and He said, "Yes. In this case, if you experimented on her it wouldn't do her any harm." He probably thought since I was going blind it wouldn't make any difference. If I recall correctly, my regular doctor came into the waiting room were I was sitting and said, "I'll see you when I get back." One day as I was praying, I felt led to read my Bible and suddenly the pages fell open to the gospel of **John 14:12-14.**

> *Verily, verily, I say unto you, He that believeth on me, the works that I do shall he do also; and greater works than these shall he do; because I go unto my Father. And whatsoever ye shall ask in my name, that will I do, that the Father may be glorified in the Son. If ye shall ask any thing in my name, I will do it.*

How wonderful and exciting! Those Scriptures came alive to me, and I realized that God's supernatural healing is for us today just like it was when Jesus was walking on earth. What a revolution in my soul. Right then Jesus gave me the faith to believe that He had touched my eyes and I was healed. My right eye was still blurry and my left eye couldn't see much at all. Before I had this revelation from God I had been to the new doctor and he had given me the new medication for my eyes, but now I know that Jesus had healed me, and with great joy I went to see this doctor again. He looked in the microscope to see into my eyes and then he got very angry and said, "The virus is still there."

My nurse became upset with the doctor, and immediately set an appointment for me with my regular eye doctor; I quickly went home. I told my husband what had happened and we prayed, and then John received from the Lord through the Holy Spirit that God never shares His Glory. That doctor could have taken all the credit for my healing, and God did not want this. I gave everything to the Lord and my faith came back stronger; I felt joy and peace again. Now was the time to see my regular eye doctor, and I hurried to his office; after he greeted me I quickly told him I was healed. He looked very strange at me, and he told me to sit down in front of the microscope. He carefully examined my eyes three times and shook his head in amazement and told me that the virus was gone, and I was healed. It didn't take long before my eyes looked perfect, and nobody could see I ever had an awful virus infection. I am very thankful to Jesus that on the cross He took all our diseases and our sorrows and all pain and afflictions.

Surely he hath borne our griefs, and carried our sorrows: yet we did esteem him stricken, smitten of God, and afflicted. But he was wounded for our transgressions; he was bruised for our iniquities: the chastisement of our peace was upon him; and with his stripes we are healed.
(Isaiah 53:4-5)

Who his own self bare our sins in his own body on the tree that we, being dead to sins, should live unto righteousness: by whose stripes ye were healed.
(1 Peter 2:24)

Highlights in Salt Lake City

Another joyful incident happened one winter when my husband was going to his job. He was backing his car out from our driveway, and he got stuck in the snow; the tires were spinning, and he couldn't get his car loose. I came out and I started to pray and laid my hands on the car. I felt the power of God move the car away from the hard snow and because of this John was able to drive to his job. Glory to God!

We had also been involved with the Gideon's. When we told them we were moving to California, they were very sad to hear about this. Yet, they knew that my husband had been accepted at the Golden Gate Baptist Seminary in Mill Valley, and they realized we were called by God to do so; they didn't want to stand in our way. Our final fellowship with them turned out to be very sweet and we loved them dearly. We would miss them very much, but we left those great people in God's care.

Chapter Seven

Moving to California

Sometime before we left for California, our church had a great dinner for us. There was wonderful fellowship. We expressed our love to them and thanked them for the years we had the privilege to know them. We cared for them greatly, and had learned a lot from the pastors and their wives. Now was the time to leave this church in Salt Lake City and begin a new life in California. A short time before the last Sunday service, John and I talked about the long trip to California, and we were concerned about driving through the desert. My husband was to drive the rental truck with all our belongings, and I was to drive our personal car. He felt it would be nice for me to have someone with me in my car. I liked this idea very much and I suggested that we pray for this, which we did.

As we went to our last service in that church we didn't know anyone who would travel to California that could possibly keep me company during our trip; but I trusted that God, who had done so many things in my life, would somehow make a way where there was no way. As our service had begun, a lady came in whom we never had seen before. The pastor welcomed her to our church and asked her where she came from. To our surprise she told him that she was a missionary who worked in Congo, Africa. She was on vacation, and she was traveling all over America; she had come from New York, and was on her way to San Francisco. She traveled by bus, had stayed overnight in Salt Lake City, and decided to go to a church before she was leaving. She looked in the phonebook and found our Church.

After the service was over we talked with her and found out that she was born in Norway. I told her where I lived in Sweden and that I had visited that country twice. We told her we were moving to a place outside San Francisco and John was driving a truck and I was driving our personal car. We asked if she would like to keep company with me in my car instead for traveling by bus. She joyfully said that she'd rather be traveling in a car and keep me company, and she looked forward to the fellowship that all three of us were going to have on our trip. What a beautiful answer to prayer! We had earlier told her that this Sunday was our last one in this church and we were ready to take off. Everything was packed. My husband went into his truck, and the Norwegian lady got situated in my car, and off we went.

It was great to hear the stories of her experiences in Africa as a missionary. She understood Swedish, and I understood Norwegian, so we had fun with that. It brought sweet memories to my mind when I was in Oslo on a vacation in 1958. In the center of this city no cars were allowed, and the police rode on horses; there were flowers all over and one could sit outside and have some good food. What an idyllic place it was. On our trip to San Francisco we all three had a wonderful fellowship as we went to eat some great food on our way to California. Before long we had arrived at our destination, which was the Golden Gate Baptist Seminary in Mill Valley. The lady from Norway saw San Francisco and then she continued to travel by bus all over America. We had earlier given her a big thank you from the bottom of our hearts. What a blessing she had been to us!

Life at the Seminary

Now we had a surprise waiting for us. When they gave us the number to the place we were going to live, we found that it was a studio apartment, which meant that we had one room and a bathroom. There was a stove and a small refrigerator. I decided to separate the room. We positioned our bookcase in such a way that it looked like we had two rooms, and then we put the table with chairs where the stove and the refrigerator were so it looked like a little kitchen. This was going to be our style of home for about three years. Many wonderful things happened there.

I got a job at Redwood Retirement Center to help out with our finances while John was going to school. This place reminded me of the place I worked at in Sweden, but less pay. My job was to assist the patients with their medication and personal needs. The boss I had on this job was a fantastic person. It was a pleasure to work for her. Later on when she had a personal tragedy I was there for her, but I wished I had been able to help her more. Her husband had been unfaithful to her when she was in the hospital having her baby, and she told me how devastated she had been; my heart went out to her as I ministered to her needs. If I recall correctly, she later was divorced.

There is one day I will never forget. It was when I had been praying for my family and friends that I heard God speak to me very clearly through the Holy Spirit, "Do not look back." Immediately I thought about Lot's wife. Genesis 19:26. I had become burdened down with my relatives, family, and friends in Sweden, when I should have concentrated more on the people here in California. The temptation was to look back but I didn't. My respect for God was much stronger. I was carrying burdens that didn't belong to me, but only to Jesus. I will never forget that powerful message that the Lord gave to me. It shook me up deep inside. I realized that Jesus had a special ministry for me right where I was. Later on at God's perfect time I was to have a ministry in Sweden.

Sharing Jesus With Others

After a while my husband and I began to do evangelistic work in different areas of California. I sang solos, and my husband did the preaching. We had a team with us: a song leader (Bill Gaddis), a pianist, and an activity leader. They were all students at the seminary, and we enjoyed these great people on our team. The song leader made a great impact on my life. He knew that I was very shy and he would introduce me to the public by saying, "Now Aina will bless you with a song." I liked it when he said this, because I wanted the people to be touched by the Holy Spirit and be blessed. Without Jesus there would be no song. He is my song and he has also given me a new song.

I thought Bill was perfect, and I was wondering if I ever could be like him. So one day when he sang, to my surprise he forgot part of the lyrics to the song. He explained to me later that his mind just went blank; he just kept on singing with a smile on his face. What a blessing he was to all of us. We visited different churches all over. One day God did a wonderful thing for us. John and I were going to a church where we had to travel by car a couple of hours from the seminary, and as we sat down in the car John realized he had lost the map and the instructions where we were going. We had never been to the place where this church was located, and there was no one we could contact at this time. I told him not to worry. I said, "I will pray and the Holy Spirit will guide me." After I had finished my prayer, the Holy Spirit came in a mighty way upon me and as John started the car, I felt God's power all over me; with the guidance of the Holy Spirit I found the place and the church.

Full Gospel Business Men's International Fellowship

When we had been at the seminary for a while we decided to go to a Full Gospel Business Men's International Fellowship Meeting. It was there the Lord confirmed to me that I had been baptized with the Holy Spirit in Salt Lake City but because we didn't have the knowledge, we didn't know what had happened to me. The church we were attending just thought I had a different salvation experience. We attended a number of conventions put on by the Full Gospel Business Men's Fellowship and we were always blessed spiritually. We were busy with our overseas crusade, and later, when my husband had graduated from Golden Gate Seminary, a church in Lodi called him to be a pastor in their church. We also did overseas meetings so we were very busy and had no contact with the Full Gospel Business Men's Fellowship at that time. Some years later John resigned from the church in Lodi, and we moved to Sacramento where he later became a pastor at Resurrection Life of Jesus Church.

Our Current Involvement With Business Men's Fellowship

Ronny Svenhard, an international director of FGBMIF, gathered a number of people to form a new organization, which was named "Business Men's Fellowship, U.S.A." We have known Ronny Svenhard since around 1970, and he and his wife have always been such a blessing to us. With the death of our good friend Joe Fry, who was the local chapter leader in Sacramento, we lost contact with the people in the organization, and did not know they had reorganized and were back in ministry again.

Over the years my husband and I had visited Kingsburg, a city in the central valley of California and a strong Swedish community. I had become good friend with June Hess, the owner of "Svenska Butiken" (Swedish Store) in Kingsburg. In the fall of 2006 I called June to ask her how she was doing. As we were talking over the phone, she told me that she had a need for an experienced Swedish baker as Swedish descendants in Kingsburg were trying to open up a Swedish restaurant.

I told June that I would like to help her; since I knew a Swedish man who has a bakery business; if he can't help maybe he would know of someone who could help her. I did not tell her the name of the man I was thinking about, but the name that came to my mind was Ronny Svenhard.

After some research I found Ronny Svenhard's business office, but I got his answering service, so I left a message on it. Later Svenhard's Director of Administration, Dian Scott, called me saying that Ronny Svenhard had asked her to call me. She also told me that the Svenhards knew June, but she had apparently never asked them

76

about a Swedish baker. I didn't know that Ronny and Norma Svenhard knew June. Dian and I had a nice talk and I told her briefly how
my husband and I had been so blessed by the Full Gospel Business
Men's meetings when we lived at the seminary in Mill Valley. The
meetings were like an oasis in the desert. It had been so refreshing to
our souls. Dian then told me about the meetings they have now, and
she sent me an invitation in the mail to their next meeting. So on Friday, October 6, 2006, we attended our first meeting in many years and
we enjoyed it very much. We met Ronny and Norma Svenhard and
also Dian Scott. We also had a chance to meet other people in lead-
ership from our area. I now had a chance to speak in person to Ronny
about the need for a Swedish baker in Kingsburg, and he told me that
he would look into it and see what he could do.

At that time we were not able to attend the Saturday morning
meeting, but we were invited back to Friday, November 3, meeting.
This time we were not only able to attend the Friday night chapter style
meeting, but also the Saturday morning convention style meeting. At
these meetings I was deeply touched by God's agape love through different people, and also I felt that the prophecy given Saturday morning was for me. God's love was coming over me in a mighty way when
we attended the meeting in December.

My Battle With Insecurity and Shyness

Earlier I had some experience with doubt about my salvation, and
it was a battle for a while, but after insight from God's Word I had great
victory over this, and out of this came a song. The lyrics came fluent-
ly in Swedish and I had an old Swedish folksong in my mind that fit with
the lyrics. Then I thought about my cousin Arne who has written songs

77

and music, plays four instruments, and plays in music bands. I thought he could be used by the Lord to write the music for my song. Happily he did it for me.

I was inspired to translate the song into English after we had moved to Sacramento. The title of the song is *Jesus Is the Way*. I did a simple sketch of how I wanted the song sheet to look, added some pictures taken at the place where I wrote the lyrics to the song, and gave it to my nephew Charles who knows about computers and also has the gift from God to put it together artistically. Later I had it copyrighted.

Chapter Eight

Tent and Revival Mettings in Sweden

Shortly before we were leaving for Sweden, I had a dream we were in a church in Stockholm. I was sitting in the middle in front of the podium; there was a choir that sang, and John was about to preach so he was also on the platform. Suddenly a lady who was singing in the choir very humbly stepped out from the choir and gave a message in tongues; my husband gave the interpretation of this. He had not had that gift before but got it on the spot. Little did I know the dream I had was prophetic. My husband did the preaching, and I testified and sang as God led me to do.

The year was 1971, and this was the time the Lord opened the door for us to go to Sweden. What a blessing it was for us to be able to go back home to share the gospel! Now we were truly born again and we had changed a lot.

John had the privilege to lead his brother Peter to the Lord, and what a joy it was for us. He was also baptized in water after a meeting in Stockholm. Then later his wife Monica also became born again. We all rejoiced about that too.

When we arrived in Sweden we found out that the Swedish Baptist Union scheduled us for meetings in Stockholm, among many other places. Later on, when we were done with the meetings, we were eager to go to Stockholm. When we came there and entered into the church where we were to be ministering, I saw the same church I had seen in my dream. Furthermore, I was placed in the middle, in front of the podium, and there was the choir singing; my husband was about to preach on the platform. Then suddenly a lady who was singing in the choir very humbly stepped out from the choir and gave a message in tongues; John gave the interpretation right on the spot. He had not had that gift before. I happened just like I saw it in the dream. How great God is.

A man came to our meetings who was a very tough man and used foul language. He had once been a sailor, but he got saved in a mighty way as we ministered to him. After a while we were going to another city in a different area and, to our surprise, they had double booked us. My husband had to do the meeting in Stockholm, and he decided that this man that had just been saved would travel with me to the other city, Linkoping, and give his testimony. I was to explain to the pastor what had happened.

We were traveling by train and everything went fine. We went to the church and later he gave his testimony. He did well considering that this was his first time. Later on there were people in the congregation who wanted to talk with me, and he also talked to some people.

After that a man from the church wanted to show us where we were to sleep for the night; this was the apartment that my husband and I were going to have. The man who had just been saved was not in that arrangement. The apartment had two rooms, a kitchen and a living room.

The man from the church left us. Right away, the man who just had been saved started to talk to me about the pastor. He was very angry. Somehow the pastor had said something to him that made him very angry, and this former sailor told me if he had the pastor here in this apartment he would decrease his airflow. In other words he would choke him. I tried very softly to explain to him this is not the way to handle a conflict with other people, but he would not pay attention at all. He was sitting in a chair and then the anointing of God came over me in a mighty way.

I realized what I had to do, and this was like having a roaring lion in front of me; an unusual courage came over me and I knelt down right in front of him and began to pray for him. Suddenly he became very quiet and as I looked upon him he looked shocked. He was not used to anything like this, and I also saw shame on his face. I had my eyes closed when I prayed so he could have hit me, but I trusted that God's power was stronger than his anger. He went to his room and I went to mine and locked it, not because of fear, but because I was exhausted and did not want any more commotion.

The next day John came back and I told him what God, through the Holy Spirit, had done. We had a good meeting, my husband preached a good sermon, and the former sailor went back to Stockholm again. The reason I shared this is to point out how important it is to always be humble, but at the same time to have faith that through

Jesus we can come boldly before the throne to our Heavenly Father. He will take care of us, and the situation. He was a big man and I was a small woman; but just like David had to face his Goliath, and had victory over him, so we can also do with the Holy Spirit's anointing. (1 Samuel 17:4-7 and 33-51).

Our Parents

Between the times when we were doing evangelistic meetings, we were able to see John's parents. We had the privilege of leading his mother to the Lord in 1973. His dad had accepted Christ as a teenager, and at this time he rededicated his life and wanted to serve God for the rest of his life. They began by helping us with the mission work in Sweden, and then later they made many visits here with us and we had some great times together. We showed them many states and places all over America; they enjoyed it very much, and learned a lot about the USA.

In 1984 they moved to Sacramento to help us in our work here. We will always be thankful for their dedication and commitment. His mother was a very generous and kind person. His dad really liked my sister-in-law Monica and me; we became his girls that he never had. I did appreciate this very much since my father was in Sweden. My husband's parents went to be with the Lord. John's father went first, in 1998. His mother went to be with the Lord in 2005. They had worked faithfully for many years in our ministry, and we will always be grateful for this.

We also had the joy of visiting with my parents, during breaks between our evangelistic meetings, when we were in their area. They were so happy to see us and we were glad to be with them. We had great times together; we took them out for dinners, and took them to different places they wanted to see. John prayed for my father for salvation and to be baptized with the Holy Spirit. I prayed for my mother for salvation and the baptism of the Holy Spirit. They attended all our meetings in the area where they lived.

Last Time to See My Dad

What wonderful days those were; we had many precious times with them. The last time John and I saw my dad was the last meeting that we had in Sweden, in 1983. My father was not well and said to me that he did not think that he would ever see me again in this life. It was the most difficult thing to say goodbye to them that I have ever experienced, but God gave me the strength to comfort them before we left. I had planned to fly back to pray for my dad but he died before I had the chance to do so.

My Last Visit With My Mother

I went to see my mother in Sweden at the Retirement Center where she lived. I decided at this time to look at our childhood home in Vedum. It was completely changed inside as well as outside. When I walked up the stairs, suddenly I was faced with many doors. I realized the house had been converted into an apartment building. On one door was a woman's name; she had the same name as my twin sister, both her first name and her last name. It gave the place a kind of strange and odd feeling. I took the stairs back down and went outside the premises.

83

Then I met my former teacher's wife. They had their home very close to our house. We had been neighbors as we were growing up, and this teacher was the best one I ever had. She invited me to come to her place. After she asked me how I was doing in America, I joyfully shared with her what was going on in our lives. Then after that we ended up having a conversation about salvation. Her husband had passed away some time earlier, and she had not read her Bible in a long time. She didn't think that she was saved, so I shared the gospel with her and led her in the sinner's prayer. She accepted Jesus Christ as her Savior. I encouraged her to read God's Word everyday. Then we said goodbye. What a wonderful day it was for me as well as for her.

I gave my mother a joyful shock when I saw her in 1991, after my father had gone to be with the Lord. My twin sister and her husband were at mother's house. My mother had been out for dinner and had just come back. I was hidden in her bedroom, and my twin sister said with a cheerful voice, "and now I have a surprise for you." I came out of the bedroom and she could barely believe her eyes when she saw me! My twin sister's husband took a video of us and later my other sister also came. That was a great day for mother when she could have all three of us girls there. She had lost a lot of weight, so I bought good food for her, and took her to places she wanted to go; I brought her a dress again from the USA which she liked very much. Slowly she regained some of her weight that she needed so much. I was happy to bring joy and comfort to her and she lived more years after my last visit. She passed to be with the Lord in 1996.

God's Beautiful Answer, on the Airplane to Sweden in 1991

This time when I was flying to Sweden, I had brought with me a small cassette player, a headset and a great music tape. After some time they were showing a movie. During this time I had been listening to the music a while, but then I looked up and saw that it was a very depressing and bad movie. Even if I hadn't looked at the movie the atmosphere was heavy with gloom and doom. I felt led by the Holy Spirit to pray to God through Jesus Christ something like this: "God, I pray that You will change this bad situation of gloom, doom, and darkness, and You will do something soon among all of us."

It wasn't very long after I had finished my prayer when suddenly the pilot spoke into the speaker system. He said to all the passengers something like this: "Excuse me for interrupting your viewing of the movie, but I want you to see something beautiful and spectacular. I didn't want you to miss it. Roll up the blinders and you will see this for yourselves." The person in charge of the movie turned it off. Soon everyone rolled up their blinders over the windows, and all the passengers, including me, were looking out through the window. What did we see? We saw a sight so striking - there are really no words to describe it. This happened in the vicinity of Greenland with the impressive icebergs. I had never seen such a fantastic sunrise before, and I had flown over Greenland many times. The sky was magnificent, and there was a bright light with beautiful colors all over the sky. One could only stand in awe of God's wonderful creation and His display of mighty colors. What an answer to prayer! (Hebrews 11:1,6). It took some time to see this, and people were walking all over to get the best view. Soon it was time to eat, and there were no more movies shown after this. God did a miracle to get the passengers' minds off the movie. Glory to God!

I have flown over the Atlantic Ocean twenty three times. I have seen a lot. I have experienced a thunderstorm with lightning outside the windows one time in an airplane. That was kind of scary. I was praying to God for a safe journey. He heard and answered that prayer. Also, when I flew with my husband on our crusade trips we had the experience of going up in an airplane in very bad fog; that was not easy, but we prayed, and by God's love and grace, we made that trip safely.

Miracles and Healings

God did many miracles during the time we had our evangelistic crusades in Sweden, Germany, Finland and Holland from 1971 to 1983. People were healed of all kinds of diseases; many were saved and baptized in water, and in the Holy Spirit. I want to share some of the highlights of the many things that God did in my life and my husband's. One day a sister in the Lord and I visited a woman who was very sick and in terrible pain. Her daughter had been to our meetings, and she wanted us to come and pray for her mother because she did not think she was saved. The reason she thought this was that her mother was never happy and she used bad language. We witnessed to her what God had done in our lives, and then we gave the plan of salvation; she prayed and asked Jesus to forgive her for her sins and to be born again. Then we cast out some ungodly spirits in her life, and prayed for Jesus to heal her and the pain to be gone. She was scheduled to go to the hospital but we believed that Jesus was going to heal her fast; we could see a change in the mother so we left their

86

place with joy. A couple of days later the daughter called me and told me that her mother was happy and joyful, and the pain she experienced was completely gone; she did not have to go the hospital. She was a new person! What a mighty God we have!

One day when I was in prayer to the Lord I had a vision of a V.W. Bug on fire, and big flames were coming out from the car. John and I were going to travel to the northern part of Sweden, and I was pondering the meaning of the vision. We took off from John's parent's place in Jonkoping and we had a long journey in front of us. After we had traveled for many miles, suddenly we saw a V.W. Bug on fire. There were some people gathered around the car. There was no one still in the car, and the driver and passengers were helped. We were happy that no one had been hurt or killed. At once a thought came into my mind, how we always have to bring the full gospel message so people can be born again before it is be too late.

Back to Mill Valley and the Seminary

The year was 1971. We had come back from Sweden and were now at the seminary again. We were still doing evangelistic outreach in different areas of California. Peter and Monica immigrated to the United States in December 1971. They first came to the seminary where we lived, and then they were able to rent an apartment in San Rafael, just some 20 minutes away from us. Together with John's brother and his wife, and some other friends, we formed our mission organization, European-American Evangelistic Crusades. Later, Peter and Monica moved to Rohnert Park. They had bought a house there, and before long they had their first child, Charles, who later moved to Sacramento. Then later on a girl was born and her name is Rachelle.

She is now married and lives outside the Santa Rosa area. Last but not the least was Joshua who was born in Sebastopol, as was Rachelle. After Charles had moved to Sacramento, Peter and Monica, and Joshua also moved to this region so that they could be closer and help us in the ministry. Not only are they helping us at the church, but they are also helping us with the mission work. Charles married Yekaterina; he now has two sons, Andrew and Isaac.

In 1972 we had invited a Swedish gospel group, Budbararna (The Messengers) whom we had come to know very well, to help us with the music in our service. We had met them in Sweden in 1971. Meetings had been set up in California and Nevada. The leader of this group was Owen Bergh, who later immigrated to the United States and is now living in the Sacramento area.

There is one meeting that stands out, which took place in the city of Stockton. My husband preached, and at the altar call many people were touched by the Holy Spirit and came forward for prayer. Later they had refreshments and a sister in the Lord and I had begun a conversation with three ladies. We decided to go to another room where it was quieter and private. One of the ladies wanted to get saved so we began to tell her how she could be born again. But then a man, Chester McMeans, came into the room where we were. Chester and his wife Dawn had set up the meeting at a Baptist Church in Stockton.

We knew he was a backslider with lots of problems. He had a crushed foot and very bad back problems with great pain. He also was a smoker. The sister in the Lord was thinking the same thing as I was, "What should we do with this man?" There was a concern, but again we both thought the same thing, that God's power was stronger than anything, so we continued with the salvation plan. To our surprise and shock, the lady collapsed and fell down on a bench. She had no heart-beat, no pulse, and she quit breathing.

There was no time to call 911, so we went immediately into intensive prayer for her life; she was raised up and was alive again. We then quickly finished the salvation plan and she received Jesus into her heart and her life. We never touched the man, but Jesus touched him and he was slain in the Spirit. When the other two ladies saw this, they also wanted to be saved, so we led them to Christ also. The conclusion was that three ladies were born again and we found out that the backslider returned to God and quit smoking. He was instantly healed of his back problem, and healed of his crushed foot. He testified all over how God had healed him. The sister in the Lord and I had a talk with each other afterwards; we found out we had thought the same thing about the whole situation. We also had the same faith to believe that Jesus Christ is the same yesterday, today, and forever. (Hebrews 13:8)

> *But Jesus beheld them, and said unto them, with men this*
> *is impossible; but with God all things are possible.*
> (Matthew 19:26)

Jesus touched not only those four people, but He touched the sister in the Lord and me with His joy and strength. I give God all honor and praise for what He did. We were just simple vessels who, in obedience, acted on the word of God.

Back in Sweden

My husband and I again traveled to Sweden and had wonderful meetings. This time we had an American gospel group with us. We had trained this group to be involved in prayer, and in witnessing. I was singing with this team. Some of them were young adults and this was the dream of their lives to be able to do evangelistic and mission work in a different country. They saw God's power in a mighty way moving as they were praying for people. The year was 1973. The gospel group's name was The New Day Singers. Chester Mc Means, who God healed from the crushed foot and other things, was with us to witness what Jesus had done in his life. His wife Dawn was in the singing group. We found out that he had been in different accidents, which explained the damage to his back and foot. He also was on strong medication because of his pain. The Lord gloriously healed him, and set him free from all his backsliding.

In May 1973, my husband graduated from the seminary with a Master of Divinity degree. I had taken some classes at the seminary, including singing and pastoral care.

Once we were there, there was a mighty move of God in the state Lutheran Church. My husband preached and gave an invitation to repent. We in the music group were singing the song *Hallelujah*. The priest went up to the altar alone and repented of his sin. Then most of the people also went to the altar, repenting of their sins. We were all very touched by it. What a mighty move by God. The love of Jesus was poured out on all those people, and I will not forget what God did in that church. This was the first time we saw a state Lutheran Church priest go forward and surrender himself to God openly in front of everyone. What a humble and fine person this man was.

My Father Plays in Our Gospel Band

In 1974 we flew back to Sweden for more meetings. This time we had a young lady with us named Paula Carpenter, and she was from the Los Angeles area. She was going to help us with working in the vacation Bible school, and also she was singing in our meetings. Paula and I sang a duet, *Do You Know My Jesus?* God was still moving in a great way. This time we were in the town of Vara, very close to where I was born. The pastor in the Pentecostal Church and my father, Helge Strom, were responsible for all information about the meetings. I shall never forget the beautiful meetings we had in Vara and the surrounding areas in my former county. In his younger days, before my father was a Christian, he used to play in a band. That was how he met my mother. He used to play mandolin or banjo. Now he was saved and very much involved with the meetings, especially in Vara. That was my desire: to have the joy to be able to hear my father play Christian music. To my surprise and great joy, he played in our music groups at the Pentecostal Church in Vara. If I recall right, I think he played the mandolin. Jesus gave me my heart's desire with that, and I had the privilege of hearing him pray a powerful prayer before the meetings. He was truly born again! What a blessing for my husband and me. To God be the glory.

Another blessing was that my cousin Arne had written the melody for my song, and in one of the meetings he accompanied me when I sang the song *"Jesus ar vagen" (Jesus is the way)*. He played the piano and sang with me in the chorus. Oh, what a move by the Holy Spirit of God. We were deeply touched over what Jesus had done in our lives. He was a former dance musician playing ungodly music, and I had danced to his orchestra many times, and now we had both become followers of Jesus Christ. John and I were also instruments of God to encourage him to be a music teacher instead of working in a factory. He had played the accordion since he was five years old, and he played by ear very well; he took the advice we gave him and quit his job in the factory to go to school to learn more theory and to write music. Later on he got a very nice job as a music teacher and is now retired but he still is playing. When I danced to his orchestra it was in the summer time in a park. The musicians were standing on a platform and playing. There was a wooden floor in the middle in which the men politely asked the ladies for a dance. In the winter I would dance in fancy restaurants, and there the ladies were treated like princesses. In this church in Vara there were sixteen people baptized in water at the end of the crusade. (Acts 8:26-38) There was a mighty move by God, and by the many testimonies and the music, and the powerful sermon, the people's lives were touched. There was a tremendous anointing by the Holy Spirit moving in our midst.

It is so wonderful to be used of God, and to see people's lives being transformed in front of your eyes; Jesus did so many great things. In 1975 we went back to Sweden for some more meetings. This time John and I were in a church named Betel, and they had given us a place where we could sleep there every night until we were done with our crusade. When I was preparing for the meeting, I had a vision: I saw a man come to this church for the evening meeting, and also to the coffeehouse. I felt led to pray for a mighty touch of God's love to be manifested. Also I knew that 1 Corinthians chapter 13 was going to be read from the Bible. Later on there was a man who did just that. My husband preached and I felt led to sing this song: "*Say Have I Done My Best for Jesus.*" The Swedish version is somewhat stronger with the lyrics. The man heard the sermon, and I saw the man that I had seen in the vision coming forward as I sang the invitation song. He surrendered his life to Jesus and he laid his cigarettes on the altar. He was a former Satan worshipper and a Nazi; after prayer, he was set free. He had been greatly touched by God. Also at that meeting was a lady who was a minister; she could not stay seated in her chair but she ran to the altar during the invitation. Jesus had mightily touched both of them. Later this man was baptized in water in a white robe. What a marvelous and touching thing we had seen. Here again we were just vessels to be used and to be obedient to do what God had told us to do. To God belongs all the honor and glory.

Chapter Nine

My Life as a Pastor's Wife

My husband accepted a call to be a pastor in Lodi in the year of 1975. He also was involved in many radio programs during this time. This was the first time for him to be a pastor, and for me to function as a pastor's wife. We learned a lot. We had rented an older house, but it was in good condition. However, the congregation wanted us to live in an apartment. They thought it would be much cheaper. So I hurried to find a townhouse apartment, which was in the right price range, and we got that. I didn't have much time to look around. We felt bad that we had rented the house. We thought it was what they had wanted us to live in because we didn't think it was that expensive.

When I separated the drapes in the kitchen and looked out, there was a swimming pool right outside our kitchen with people walking outside, men and women in their skimpy swimsuits, and I closed the drapes very fast. This was not very uplifting so I went to the Lord in prayer. He spoke to me that one day you will have your own house, and I believed Him. After we had lived there for a short while I found another apartment on the second floor. It was not a fancy place but it was clean and the price on the rent was right. We had been in Lodi about two years when John felt led by the Lord to resign as a pastor from Lodi Christian Life Center.

God gave me a message and a sign: "When the myrtle tree outside your window has finished blooming you will be moving to Sacramento." We just had to pray and wait on God to carry this out through the Holy Spirit, and believe in faith that He would guide us.

It happened exactly the way He had revealed it to me. When the time came for us to move to Sacramento, I was carefully cleaning our apartment to leave it in good shape when I finally came to clean the oven. Suddenly the door to the oven fell out from its hinges. John and I tried to put it back as we prayed, but it didn't work. John had to go to the Post Office before they closed. So he was in a hurry to go.

After he left, I realized this was a very old and difficult construction. It dawned on me that we had gone in the flesh, in our own strength; we had cried out to Jesus for help, but we had not waited for Him to speak to us. So I began to pray that Jesus, by the Holy Spirit, would show me exactly how I should put the door back in its right position. I had to do certain movements with my hands, and then I got the oven door back where it should be.

Thanks to God to whom I give all the praise. I was just a vessel who believed that He would see me through because of faith in Jesus Christ, working by the Holy Spirit to guide me. John had thought that he was going to have to talk to the landlord about the situation when he got home, but as soon as I heard his car coming, I ran down to meet him and I told him, "You don't need the landlord. Come up and see for yourself!" When he came into the kitchen he saw the oven door back where it belonged and he could almost not believe what his eyes had seen. But the fact remains that Jesus used me that day in a mighty way by the Holy Spirit.

One day as I was praying, I had a vision: I had a pencil in my right hand and it wrote one word: *write*. I had never had anything like this happen to me before, so I was praying for God to show me. After we had moved to Sacramento and had moved into our new apartment, I had the same vision again. I was pondering what this was all about. Did God want me to write a poem, a song, or a story? The third and last time the same vision appeared was when we were in Los Angeles. We had gone to a Full Gospel Business Men's meeting and instead of us staying in a hotel we stayed with friends, Sam and Kitty Yarkin, in their home. It was there that I got the final vision. I shared the vision with Kitty and she was much exited about it. I shared the vision with a pastor, Sam Mushegan, whom John and I had known for a long time, and he felt joy and peace about it. This had to do with my writing my story.

A long time passed since I had the first vision, but one day I was led to sit down by my typewriter. I prayed that God would show me what to write. When I began to write, my thoughts came about my childhood and what happened to me after this. As I began this writing, it was very short, the reason was I thought it was only to be a testimony and there was not room enough in our Dove magazine at that time.

Moving to Sacramento

We started some Bible studies in different homes in the Sacramento area, and God was blessing our efforts. We also did some evangelistic work in other areas. We did another trip to Sweden, and God was with us. This was 1977.

In the fall of 1978, a non-denominational church called Christian Life Ministries was formed in Sacramento with my husband as its first pastor. In 1979 it became evident that God was leading the church to stop the daily radio programs with John on KCVR in Lodi, and to switch to a new station in Carmichael, called KFIA. I had the privilege of sharing my personal testimony there, as well as on TV.

Another Trip to Sweden and Finland

This was also in 1979 when we took with us Wid and Marion Coryell on our travels to Denmark, Sweden, and Finland. Wid had the gift of leading people into praise with a happy smile on his face. God had also given Marion a beautiful voice; she was a counselor, and involved with prayer. Owen Bergh was with us in most of our meetings. He has been a leader in several gospel groups including the group he had when they were here in California. He is a gifted guitar player. Later on he moved from Sweden and married Irene and they are both living in California. Marion had her roots in Denmark, and she was so happy that in her travels with us she was able to see her beloved Copenhagen. I shall never forget when we were in Finland and John lost his voice completely. When he began his sermon he could only wheeze out some words; Owen read from the Bible, and we on the team prayed without ceasing for John. Suddenly his voice came back in full strength. This healing took place in Helsinki. Praise

98

the Lord.

In 1980 I had a vision of a map of a town that I had never been to, Karleby in Finland. We had met a man from the northern part of Sweden and had corresponded with him. We asked him if he knew this place, and to my joy, he wrote back and gave me the information that his mother lived in that place, and he felt that the vision was from the Lord. He was going to arrange for meetings in this place, which he did. What a marvelous blessing.

One day I had been praying to Jesus for a need that we had. I didn't tell anyone about this; it was a private thing. We received money for our travel expenses, food, and a place to stay. During the invitation a lady came up to the altar and she put something in my hand; I saw it was a good sum of money. I told her that we don't accept any money for ministering to people but she looked so sad; she told me the Lord had told her to give this money to me, and she insisted I take it. Then I realized the Lord had told this woman to do this. She had no clue that I had prayed a special prayer for our needs.

The Crash With Our Van

We had many answers to our prayers when we were traveling with our van all over, but especially in the northern part of Sweden. One time our lives were spared when a big truck and a small car passed us and we had snow walls on both sides of the road. It truly was a miracle. They passed us at the same time. Another time in the evening our headlights were as candlelight, and we had to use a flashlight until we arrived at our final destination. Another time we had to travel a long way from the southwest to the northern part of Sweden, and we had a late start. We had been driving for a long time, and I felt led to tell my husband to drive slower, but he felt we were doing fine. After some time I had another leading for him to drive slower, but he told me I shouldn't be concerned and the road looked real good even if there was snow on both sides of the road. There was no snow on the road.

Finally, I felt a very strong urge to give him a final warning. I felt very uneasy and told him to slow down. He said that people are waiting for us, and it is already late. Then suddenly he hit black ice and I had only time to pray, "Jesus help." He lost control of the van and it went like a sleigh on the road. It turned upside down. When we came to, my husband was under me and I was hanging by my seatbelt. He was able to reach the ignition key to turn off the motor. In a very calm voice, I asked him if he was hurt and he said he wasn't. He asked how I was doing, and I said I was fine. He was able to crawl up where I was. We tried to open the door but we couldn't. Then I prayed and took dominion over the door, and for the door to open in the name of Jesus. Suddenly it flew wide open.

We were then able to get out and look at the situation. The door at the driver's side was bent, but it could be fixed. It was a miracle we had come out of this accident alive. We also had four more miracles. Close by the road were some big rocks the van could have hit, and also there were some phone poles very near. Besides this, it was God's grace that at that time there were no cars coming. The next miracle was that there was long knife lying on top of one of our boxes where we had all of our Bible study books. My husband had brought his toolbox with him, and that knife could have hit one of us during the time of the accident.

We were very thankful there was a farm located near the scene of

100

the accident. We took a walk up to the house and knocked on the door. When the man opened the door, we told him about our accident.

This was late in the evening, and his wife and children were asleep, but he was very friendly and went out to see our van; we went back to the farm house and made a call to our friends, and the man of the house called for help to get our van up on the road. Soon a tow truck driver came and turned the van upright. All the boxes laid in a mess in the back of the van. We thanked God for his mercy and grace, and then we drove very slowly to our friends. We were very exhausted when we finally arrived there. I had been very calm when my husband was somewhat shocked immediately after the accident, but on our way to our friends I had the feeling of going off the road; I had a difficult time the rest of the way, but after we had prayed I was able to get over that terrible feeling.

The Ice Breaker

One time when we were on a ferry going to Finland we got stuck in the ice. On the ferry there were some people that were not sober, and they were hollering that now we are going to stay here the rest of the night. There was such unbelief; it was like a thick cloud. I was praying that God in His mercy would either do a miracle, or send an icebreaker. I had never seen an icebreaker in action so I didn't mind that at all; about 2-3 hours later, a huge icebreaker came to our rescue. What a sight to behold how he broke that ice and just pulverized it in front of our eyes. After we broke loose from the ice, the ferry took us to Finland without any more problems. What a beautiful answer to prayer. I am thinking right now as I write this about a line of a song that would fit what happened. This is how it goes, "Prayer is the key to heaven but faith unlocks the door."

My Former Sunday School Teacher

My heart was deeply touched, and at the same time very humbled, when in Sweden I was asked to pray for my childhood Sunday school teacher. After we had finished the meeting in my home county, my Aunt Elvira came to me and said, "I have your Sunday school teacher here and she wants you to pray for her to be baptized in the Holy Spirit, and to receive the gift that would edify her and help her to minister better to other people." When greeting her, I was thinking to myself, "How I can pray for her?" I felt unworthy since she had been my teacher, and had been a follower of Jesus for so long. I felt that I didn't have the gift to do what she was asking. But then I thought, "Who am I that I should say no to her? If she has faith that when I pray for her God will provide this gift, then I should not hinder the work of the Holy Spirit." She had gone to many people who had prayed for her, but she never received this gift of speaking in tongues. I humbly prayed for her that she would receive this precious gift from God through Jesus Christ, and instantly she received the Baptism of the Holy Spirit. God showed me clearly His power is unlimited, as long as I have faith and love for the person, and I am obedient to the Lord, through the Holy Spirit.

Reinert's Surrender to God

As I was praying one day in 1983, God spoke to me to fast for Reinert, my husband's best friend who had been in our wedding. We had witnessed to him and his wife through the years, and now he was writing to us that he would come and visit us here in the USA. I got a message from God that before he would leave America to return to Sweden, he would be saved. I didn't know how, or where. Before long he was on his way, and we picked him up at the airport here. The three of us drove to our home in Sacramento. During his time here I could see how God was working in his life.

One time we decided to do some camping and the weather began to change. It was raining, so Reinert and my husband, decided to drive back home. I was sitting in the car and silently praying. The Holy Spirit caused me to look at one of the maps we had in the car and I saw a place where we had never been before. It was Yosemite. God spoke through the Holy Spirit that there was sunshine there and lovely weather. I then spoke to my husband that I had been praying and God had told me by His Holy Spirit we should drive toward this place. They realized I had received something that was of God, so we packed our things and took off. As we were driving higher up through the mountains we saw the most spectacular view we had ever seen. Reinert was amazed over what he saw, and John and I were marveling over God's beautiful creation. The weather was beautiful, and we stayed there for a short time. Then we went back to Sacramento, since it was now Sunday morning, and we were all going to our church,

I was looking forward to what God was going to do in Reinert's life. I kind of thought he might go to the altar after my husband's preaching, and during the invitation I was praying along with other people who knew that Reinert was not saved. To our sorrow he didn't go to the altar. We went home to eat our dinner, and after this John had an engagement; he felt led to have Reinert and I listen to a tape he had just made of preaching in Swedish. I had always prayed for those tapes he sent, and had listened to every tape. However, this time I had not had time to listen. After John took off for the church, and Reinert and I had finished listening to the tape, I asked Reinert if he had any questions. He said that he did. So we went to the kitchen and I grabbed hold of my Bible and papers. At 6:00 p.m. we were to be at the church, so I began to read from the Bible, and shared some Bible verses that had to do with his salvation. Then he began to cry, and said, "It is too late for me. I didn't go to the altar." He cried like his heart was broken apart. It was then I knew that I was it, and the Holy Spirit came over me in such a mighty way. I told him it is never too late with God, and then I led him to say the sinner's prayer. He got saved! I also talked about how to be baptized in water and to be baptized in the Holy Spirit. What a joy! We then left and took off for the church. We arrived there a little bit late, but in perfect time for Reinert to testify what God had done through the Holy Spirit. John and Reinert hugged each other, and I felt like dancing with joy. I have to say that in my flesh, I felt awkward about leading a man to the Lord, but the Holy Spirit helped me all the way even if it was a very rare situation for me. I am quoting Reinert's own words from our guest book:

"When I came to USA to visit you I couldn't dream that I would some weeks later be saved, get baptized in the Holy Spirit and be baptized in water. To live among people who were led by God's Spirit caused me to surrender my life to God."

We Have No Problems

In 1984 my husband and I went to see our friend Dennis Sheehan who lived in San Jose, and we also went to James Robison's meetings. My husband and I had experienced a church split for the first time in our lives, and it was very painful to us. It was so bad that John and I decided to spend some time alone with fasting and prayer as we traveled to a place up in the mountains, and God spoke to my husband that we were to leave that church. We were also to go back and pick up the equipment that belonged to our organization. Needless to say, our hearts were broken. So we needed some encouragement. I had been listening to James Robison preach on television for some time, and had been corresponding with him. I had also heard his personal testimony how he was set completely free. It was also a special blessing to hear his wife's testimony. I was deeply touched by their ministry, and I found out they were going to have meetings in San Jose. I talked to John about going, and he was all for it. So we called Dennis and he also thought it was a great idea. He had experienced a bad situation with somebody about his finances, and he was heartbroken about that; when we arrived at his place we shared our situation with him, and he felt really bad about that. We went to the meetings and they were great, but my husband and Dennis kind of had a shipwreck in their faith.

In my case, I had very much taken care of it and had given everything to God. So my faith was soaring, and I exhorted them. I felt led to say to them they should call James Robison, and ask for an appointment with him and share what we all had gone through. They thought he probably is too busy, and he would be hard to get in touch with. This looked impossible to them at the time, but I didn't feel led to give up on this. I said, "Why don't you at least try?" John took a look at me and decided to call. Lo and behold, who answered the phone? It was James Robison himself, no secretary, but him. My husband was absolutely taken by total surprise, but he managed to ask for an appointment with him. James Robison said something like this: "Why don't we have some lunch together and talk." By now John realized that God had been directing me as I walked in faith. When my husband told our story, James Robison answered, "This should not have happened." He looked very concerned, and his wife Betty looked at us with great love on her face. I took courage and asked James Robison if he thought God had called John to be an evangelist instead of a pastor. He said this is very much possible. Now comes the funny part. James Robison asked Dennis, "What is your problem?" Dennis realized by now James Robison had not encountered such a thing, and didn't really know how to deal with this. Dennis said, "I have no problems!" Then our luncheon was over and James Robison invited us to a special meeting for only a small group of people; he had some nice teaching and we went back to Dennis' apartment. If I recall it correctly, John was making a joke with Dennis and he said, "I have no problems." We all started to laugh and carried on with, "We have no problems!" The good part of it all was they were no longer depressed, and we saw the humor in it. Later on I heard James Robison on television ask for forgiveness if he had hurt any one's feelings; he explained he had not done much personal ministry. He was speaking to the masses, but I thought that was very great of him to say that. Praise God! By the way, we never felt hurt by James Robison.

My husband resigned as a pastor for Christian Life Ministries in 1984 and then worked as an evangelist and Bible teacher. In 1985 God called him to start a new church in the Sacramento area, which was given the name Resurrection Life of Jesus Church. My husband is still the pastor of this church as of 2007.

As you can see from my story, we have many spiritual children, but we have no children of our own. Although we love children dearly, it was very difficult for us and especially for me on mother's day. I dreaded that day every time; but then one Sunday in the church at mother's day, I was guided by the Holy Spirit to pray for all the mothers, and as I prayed a special blessing for each one I had victory over my own emotions. After the church service was over, to my surprise and joy, all the sisters in the Lord gave me a beautiful bouquet of flowers and said, "You have helped and nourished many spiritual children so you are a mother, and you deserve those flowers just like us." This is my recollection of what happened that day.

One thing that stands out in my mind, that is very touching, is that we had had a young couple who had two children, and my husband and I loved them all very much. They had a boy and a girl. The boy was five years old and the girl three; they were very special to us. They were very well behaved, and obedient to their parents. It was obvious that their parents loved them. The boy would ask John and me many questions about spiritual things - he seems to be much older than he was. He and his little sister were always talking about Jesus all the time.

Their parent's names were Steve and Zondra. After a few years they decided to attend another church, and the children must have heard their parents talking about it. At that time we did not know they were leaving. At the last time in the church I shall never forget when they said goodbye to us.

The parents and the little girl hugged us and the boy hugged my husband before me. Then the boy jumped up on me and hugged me.

He held on to me for dear life, a long time. Finally he let go of me and they left.

My First Family Visit

We also had the joy of having my twin sister Daga, and her husband Rolf, pay us a visit in 1987. We had a great time showing them places all over California. They were also able to be with us in one of our services at the church. They were very thankful and happy for everything we did for them. It was difficult to say goodbye to them at the airport. We were happy they made it safely back to Sweden.

In the year of 1996 I wrote my story, but I felt it was not complete. I wanted to give some highlights of my travel overseas, and also about our work here in America in the evangelistic field, our mission work and church work here. When God spoke to me the first time, in Lodi, that I was to write, I began to type on my typewriter in obedience. It seems to me that the Holy Spirit wanted for me to write about my childhood and my personal life. So I did. Now I am completing my life story, before and after I was saved.

Another Visit

In 1998 my sister Vally and her husband Lennart came and visited us. It was nice to see them again. We also showed them many things here in California like we had done with my twin sister and her husband. They also wanted to see the Grand Canyon, and we ourselves had not seen this place. We were happy to take them there, and when we had arrived, we were in awe how beautiful and magnificent this area was.

They also wanted to see our church. They went with us and heard the praise music and most of the sermon, but unfortunately they had to catch the airplane back to Sweden; our Swedish friend Owen drove them to the airport. It was a sad goodbye, but we were thankful they made the trip back to Sweden safely. We have witnessed to them over the years, but they have not accepted Jesus Christ as Lord and Savior into their lives yet. However, we are still praying for my sisters and their families, as well as other relatives and friends.

Unshackled

When my husband and I were living at the Seminary, we traveled all over California and other places on our free weekends. We ministered to many people. We often put on the radio and listened to the program *Unshackled*. This program was sent from Chicago, and they have a worldwide gospel outreach, and a vital ministry to Chicago's homeless. It is called Pacific Garden Mission. *Unshackled* is a radio drama, using only true stories. Little did I know at that time in my life, one day I would myself be on that program.

It was not until we had moved to the Sacramento area that I felt led by the Holy Spirit to send my personal testimony to the Pacific Garden Mission in 1998. I gave much prayer to see if it was God's will for me to be on the program. At first I was not sure if I should have this recording made because when I was an unbeliever I had fooled around with acting and with imitating actors. But then I read some Bible verses that gave me courage to send in my story. (I Corinthians 9:19 and Galatians 3:26-29)

Then it happened. The year was now 1998. They wrote me back and I had to answer a lot of questions; I had to prove to them that I was the person I claimed to be. I had to give them details about my grand-parents and my family, plus pictures and many more things. Then they accepted me. They sent me the script to check on names if they were spelled right. I only made a few changes in the story, and then I sent it back to them. The coordinator was a beautiful person, and I was pleased to have her. It took them altogether nine months to finish my story. One Christian actor playing me in the drama broke her leg, and had to sit in a certain position. It must have been difficult.

When everything was done, they told me the date and time when my story would be performed. It was quite touching when John and I heard my story, which of course included John. It brought tears to my eyes seeing how God had touched my life and done so many won-derful things, with me being a very shy and quiet young lady, very inse-cure and not knowing how to speak English. They were nice to send me a tape of my story plus other people's testimonies with their true stories that had also gone out all over the world. Now my sisters and my cousin and his family have heard my testimony.

I believe God told me to write my personal story as a testimony so I would have this to send to the Pacific Garden Mission, and so I could be on their program "Unshackled." Now they have their stories on CD. There was one thing I know for sure, and that is God had given me much courage, and in myself I was also very adventurous, not willing to give up easily.

A Bicycle Accident

God is still working in our lives with miracles. We are also praying for a continuing revival in our lives, and in this country. I also want to tell you that in the midst of miracles, we also have trials and heartache.

Not too long ago, I had an accident and fell very badly resulting in a fracture on my right hand. My arm got badly hurt, and I am very right handed. I was determined to complete this story even if it was not easy to do. So with my arm in a splint, I picked the letters with my left hand. The pain was very bad, but God helped me to be able to do it and I thank the Lord I am now able to write with both hands. Glory to God. I am thankful I didn't give in to the enemy, even in my pain.

And ye shall know the truth and the truth shall make you free.

(John 8:32)

May I give this exhortation to anyone that reads this story? Do not let pride, shyness, or fear hinder you from coming to Jesus. I lost many precious years of my life and had to go through a lot of heartaches before I got saved. *Today is the day of salvation;* tomorrow could be too late. Not only have I accepted Christ, but also I have been set free from all kinds of bondage. I'm free from the traditions of men, and have destroyed all the occult and the ungodly things in my life. (Exodus 20:3-6; 2 Chronicles 34:1-4)

Jesus will soon come back for His bride. Are you ready to meet him? Only those that have accepted Jesus as savior and Lord into their lives and into their hearts with full repentance will be saved. (John 3:16; Acts 3:19; Luke 12:37-40 and I Thessalonians 4:16-18)

And many that believed came, and confessed, and showed their deeds. Many of them also which used curious arts brought their books together, and burned them before all men: and they counted the price of them, and found it fifty thousand pieces of silver. So mightily grew the word of God and prevailed.

(Acts 19:18-20)

111

Thou shalt have no other gods before me.

Thou shalt not make unto thee any graven image, or any likeness of any thing that is in heaven above, or that is in the earth beneath, or that is in the water under the earth: thou shalt not bow down thyself to them, nor serve them: for I the Lord thy God am a jealous God, visiting the iniquity of the fathers upon the children unto the third and fourth generation of them that hate me; and showing mercy unto thousands of them that love me, and keep my commandments.

(Exodus 20:3-6)

I waited patiently for the Lord; and he inclined unto me, and heard my cry. He brought me up also out of a horrible pit, out of the miry clay, and set my feet upon a rock, and established my goings. And he hath put a new song in my mouth, even praise unto our God: many shall see it, and fear, and shall trust in the Lord. Blessed is that man that maketh the Lord his trust, and respecteth not the proud, nor such as turn aside to lies.

(Psalm 40:1-4)

Jesus put a "new song in my mouth."

A Song of Thanksgiving

Behold, God is my salvation; I will trust, and not be afraid: for the Lord JEHOVAH is my strength and my song; he also is become my salvation.

Therefore with joy shall ye draw water out of the wells of salvation? And in that day shall ye say, Praise the Lord, call upon His name, declare his doings among the people, make mention that His name is exalted.

Sing unto the Lord; for He hath done excellent things: this is known in all the earth. Cry out and shout, thou inhabitants of Zion: for great is the Holy One of Israel in the midst of thee.

(Isaiah 12:2-6)

Salvation Plan

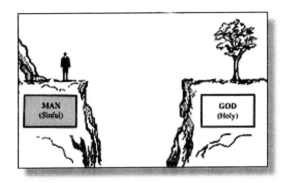

Do you know where you will go when you die? There are millions of people going to hell and they don't even know it. You might have some questions regarding Christianity and what it is exactly that makes a person a Christian. How does a person get to heaven? Does God have a standard; and if He does, what is it? Your future in eternity will depend on the decision you make! Please take the time to read God's plan of salvation; it will be the most important decision you will ever make!

Acknowledge you are a sinner who needs to be saved and that you cannot save yourself.

For all have sinned, and come short of the glory of God.
(Romans 3:23)

But God commends his love toward us, in that while we were yet sinners, Christ died for us.
(Romans 5:8)

For the wages of sin is death: but the gift of God is eternal life, through Jesus Christ our Lord.
(Romans 6:23)

For by grace are you saved, through faith; and that not of yourselves: it is the gift of God: Not by works lest any man should boast. For we are his workmanship, created in Christ Jesus to good works, which God has before ordained that we should walk in them.
(Ephesians 2:8-10)

Believe that God loves you and desires to forgive you, believe that Jesus Christ is the Son of God and that He is the only way to heaven.

For God so loved the world, that he gave his only begotten Son, that whosoever believeth in him should not perish, but have everlasting life. For God sent not his Son

into the world to condemn the world; but that the world through him might be saved.

(John 3:16-17)

Jesus saith unto him, I am the way, the truth, and the life: no man cometh unto the Father, but by me.

(John 14:6)

For whosoever shall call upon the name of the Lord shall be saved.

(Romans 10:13)

If my people, which are called by my name, shall humble themselves, and pray, and seek my face, and turn from their wicked ways; then will I hear from heaven, and will forgive their sin, and will heal their land.

(2 Chronicles 7:14)

And be ye kind one to another, tenderhearted, forgiving one another, even as God for Christ's sake hath forgiven you.

(Ephesians 4:32)

Confess and repent to God of your sins, tell Him that you are sorry and want to be forgiven.

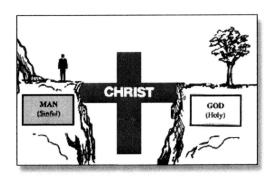

117

If we confess our sins, he is faithful and just to forgive us our sins, and to cleanse us from all unrighteousness.

(1 John 1:9)

That if you shall confess with your mouth the Lord Jesus, and shall believe in your heart that God has raised him from the dead, you shall be saved. For with the heart man believes unto righteousness; and with the mouth confession is made unto salvation. For the scripture says, Whosoever believes on him shall not be ashamed. For there is no difference between the Jew and the Greek: for the same Lord over all is rich unto all that call upon him. For whosoever shall call upon the name of the Lord shall be saved.

(Romans 10:9-13)

If you read this and realize that you are hopelessly lost, that there is nothing you can do to earn your way into heaven, all that remains to do is to ask God to save you. If you ask, God will answer!

Dear Lord Jesus, forgive me of my sins, cleanse my heart of all sin and wickedness, come in to my life and be my Lord and Savior. I believe you shed your precious blood on the cross; you died and rose again on the third day for me. Save me Jesus, I know I can't save myself. Thank you for giving me eternal life and a place in heaven with you. Amen.

Remember this, what Jesus has done in the past; He will do in the future. If you call out to Him, He will answer you. What He will do for one person, He will do for another. God is not a respecter of persons and He doesn't show favoritism. He will help anybody who calls out to Him; *you can take that to the bank!*

If you just went through the ABC's of salvation and asked Jesus to save you, you are now a Christian! The Bible says in Romans 10:13, *"For whosoever shall call upon the name of the Lord shall be saved."* Thus you are saved, not because you might feel saved, but because you have called upon God and He has saved you. Now, as a way to grow closer to Him, the Bible tells you to follow up on your commitment:

Spend time with God each day. It does not have to be a long period of time. Just develop the daily habit of talking with Him and reading the Bible. Ask God to increase your faith and your understanding of the Bible.

Find a local church where you can worship God and seek fellowship with other Christians to answer your questions and support you. Be sure they use a King James Bible if you live in an English speaking country and that the Pastor teaches from the Bible.

Also, don't forget to share your new faith in Jesus with someone else.

Please contact us and share the good news! We will send you some written material that will help you in your new walk with Jesus. Write us at P.O. Box 41001, Sacramento, Ca. USA 95841